PRAISE FOR

Lowestoft Chronicle

"*Lowestoft Chronicle* presents entertaining and exciting stories that lend themselves toward travel without dipping completely over into travel writing." —Kirsten McIlvenna, Newpages.com

"Armchair travelers, rejoice! *Lowestoft Chronicle* brings the far corners of the world to the reader's armchair. The stories and poems vary in tone from dead serious to delightful whimsy, offering something for every taste."

—Mary Beth Magee, Examiner.com

"Travel writers, here's a great place for your work. A tip of the hat (sombrero, fez) to *Lowestoft Chronicle* for fueling our urge to turn off *Jersey Shore*, toss our cell phones into a lake, and go embrace this amazing planet of ours. Bon Voyage!" —Franz Wisner, *New York Times* bestselling author of *Honeymoon with My brother*

"Go ahead, read it right now. I'll wait… Fun, huh? Thought it might pep up your midweek. All things considered, it might just be a very good thing if the *Lowestoft Chronicle* were to achieve their goal of world domination. Best wishes to them!" —Cheryl LaGuardia, *Library Journal*

"Something to check out when you just want to read. They even have a print version…wonderful little collections of short stories and essays. It's worth a look for fans of short stories, creative non-fiction and poetry."

—Dave Dempsey, Radio FM4

"It's unique and the quality of the writing is amazingly high. Highest praise: it made me want to write short stories again."

—Luke Rhinehart, internationally bestselling author of *Matari, Long Voyage Back* and *The Dice Man*

"Full of great talent and exceptionally well written pieces. An entertaining read." —Tara Smith, *The Review Review* (5-Star Review)

"*Lowestoft Chronicle* is a wonderful new addition to the world of creative writing." —Tony Perrottet, acclaimed author of *The Naked Olympics*

"A fun read." —*New York Journal of Books*

"*Lowestoft Chronicle* is a standout among a growing universe of online journals. Every issue delivers a cornucopia of entertaining and thought-provoking stories and articles." —Michael C. Keith, acclaimed author of *The Next Better Place*

"A brilliant, savory, sharp, amusing and varied taste of my favorite magazine, *Lowestoft Chronicle*. I'm delighted that a place exists for this kind of travel writing. Nicholas Litchfield has put together something very special, something to celebrate, enjoy, savor."

—Jay Parini, internationally bestselling author of
The Last Station and *The Passages of H.M.*

"The *Lowestoft Chronicle* is both classy and fun to read. A work accomplished by careful attention to detail and quality."

—Sheldon Russell, award-winning author of
Dreams to Dust and the Hook Runyon mystery series

"Terrific anthology. The writing here is fresh, surprising, and alive. If you aren't familiar with *Lowestoft Chronicle*, head on over there. They publish, on a consistent basis, excellent fiction, poetry, and non-fiction."

—Nicholas Rombes, author of
A Cultural Dictionary of Punk: 1974-1982

"I'm always impressed with the quarterly online literary magazine, *Lowestoft Chronicle*—it's filled with intriguing fiction, non-fiction, poetry, and interviews." —Matthew P. Mayo, Spur Award-winning author of
Tucker's Reckoning and *Stranded*

"Nicholas Litchfield's selection of stories, poems, memoirs and interviews is a treasure for readers who enjoy a good dose of humor with their armchair travel." —Mary Donaldson-Evans, author of *Madame Bovary at the Movies* and *Medical Examinations*

"This is the only literary magazine I read these days, and it's always enjoyable. It takes the reader to a wide variety of literary destinations, and makes even a confirmed hermit like me want to get up and go somewhere. Highly recommended." —James Reasoner, *New York Times* bestselling author

"Reading *Lowestoft Chronicle* is like jostling through a sprawling bazaar in Tashkent or Ulaanbaatar, with eyes wide open and wits on high alert. Invigorating, too." —Victor Robert Lee, author of *Performance Anomalies*

"*Lowestoft Chronicle* publishes some of the finest work of travel writing on the Internet today." —Krystal Sierra, *The Review Review* (5-Star Review)

"The much-admired *Lowestoft Chronicle* [is] an eclectic and innovative online journal. Packed into the pages are stories to entice, enthral, and entertain… incisive and enlightening interviews…[and] a tasty blend of pleasing and deftly prepared poems." —Pam Norfolk, *Lancashire Post*

"How did I not know about the *Lowestoft Chronicle*? If you're late to this travel and literary parade as well, check out Nicholas Litchfield's superb online journal specializing in all things to do with travel, literature, and the overlap between these life-nourishing activities."

—James R. Benn, acclaimed author of
the Billy Boyle World War II mystery series

"A powerful literary passport—this adventurous anthology is all stamped up with exciting travel-themed writing. With humor, darkness, and charm, its lively prose and poetry will drop you into memorable physical and psychological landscapes. Pack your bags!"

—Joseph Scapellato, acclaimed author of
Big Lonesome and *The Made-Up Man*

"The literary equivalent of Rick's Café in *Casablanca*, where travelers of all stripes pull up a stool and swap stories at the bar. Handsomely designed and expertly curated, *Lowestoft Chronicle* drives us into the arms of experience."   —Scott Dominic Carpenter, acclaimed author of
Theory of Remainders

"In this quarterly, you'll find creative nonfiction, short stories, and a few poems, with a welcome dose of humor in many. Wander around the site and you'll find intriguing stories."   —Pat Tompkins, Afar.com

"*Lowestoft Chronicle* is contemporary and worldly but with a sepia charm. It's a Baedeker for the vicarious traveler in the age of globalization."

—Ivy Goodman, award-winning author of
Heart Failure and *A Chapter from Her Upbringing*

"A solid collection of funny and fine travel-themed stories, poetry, essays and interviews that easily fits in a back pocket or carry-on bag."

— Frank Mundo, Examiner.com

"An impressive collection of travel works that sweeps the reader across the globe. The characters here, though sometimes lost in distant lands and curious customs, never fail to be lost in wonder. Here is your ticket to travel with them, to lose yourself in these pages, to satisfy your inner nomad."

—Dorene O'Brien, award-winning author of
Voices of the Lost and Found

"Three attributes of a good literary journal are variety, quality, and the unexpected. *Lowestoft Chronicle* supplies all three."

—Robert Wexelblatt, award-winning author of
Zublinka Among Women

"A wonderful collection from a fine literary journal. Fine writing that stirs the imagination, often amuses and always entertains."

—Dietrich Kalteis, award-winning author of
Ride the Lightning and *Zero Avenue*

THE VICARIOUS TRAVELER

A LOWESTOFT CHRONICLE ANTHOLOGY

Books in the Lowestoft Chronicle Anthology Series

THE VICARIOUS
TRAVELER

A LOWESTOFT CHRONICLE ANTHOLOGY

EDITED BY NICHOLAS LITCHFIELD

FOREWORD BY MICHAEL C. KEITH

Lowestoft
Chronicle
Press

THE VICARIOUS TRAVELER

SUBMISSIONS

The editors welcome submissions of poetry and prose. For submission information please visit our website at www.lowestoftchronicle.com or email: submissions@lowestoftchronicle.com

Published by Lowestoft Chronicle Press, Cambridge, Massachusetts
www.lowestoftchronicle.com

First edition: October 2019

Cover and book design by Tara Litchfield

ISBN 13: 978-1-7323328-1-2
ISBN 10: 1-7323328-1-9

Printed in the United States of America

CONTENTS

INTERVIEW

CREATIVE NON-FICTION

CONTRIBUTORS | 192
COPYRIGHT NOTES | 202

FOREWORD
Michael C. Keith

The annual publication of the *Lowestoft Chronicle Anthology*, edited by Nicholas Litchfield, has become a much-anticipated event because each new issue constitutes a special gift to the reader—a literary gem to be savored. There are a host of reasons why this is true, foremost among them the exceptional variety of travel and adventure themes coupled with high-quality writing. As expected, this latest incarnation of the publication stays the course with the best works of prose and poetry appearing in the quarterly online magazine over the past year. I found many yarns and fables in this collection thoroughly engaging. In fact, the lead off entry serves as a fine example.

In his cautionary tale, "Surf's Up!," Rob Dinsmoor aptly depicts two very distinct worlds—one on the cusp of destruction (due to the grim impact of sudden and profound climate change) and the other (an adolescent's universe) where nothing is so serious that fun is deferred. Here, the surf's being *up* means the jig is up for the human race. We chuckle nervously at the end of the narrative when the naïve protagonist (a teenager who has chosen to stay behind when her parents head north and shelter in place for the post-apocalyptic times afoot) texts her father, "It's a whole new world down here. Savage, but oh so pretty…"

On the non-fiction side of the ledger, an equally thought-provoking (albeit in a more humorous, less darkly portentous way) account, "The Priority Line" by David McPherson, relates the misadventures of the author as he stands in the wrong line at the airport. "I found myself boxed in by priority passengers in front and behind me," writes McPherson. "I was conspicuously out of place among the silk scarves and designer shoes—I clearly didn't belong."

While many of us don't have the wherewithal to qualify for the *priority* line, this astute and witty depiction does. It has earned its elevated status through what good writing is designed to achieve—relatability. It connects to its reader—the legions of us at the mercy of our unenviable financial situation.

> When my time came, the gate agent looked at me in line and held up her hand like a traffic cop. She knows! She walked toward me. I had the urge to run. My heart was pounding.

In addition to a cache of richly hewn improvisations and factual reflections, the anthology possesses a generous serving of elegant verse. "Fisherman" poignantly portrays the sublime commonality (brotherhood) of men whose lives are literally and deliberately spent "on line" (of the fishing pole variety) and "Passport Control" where lines (of the queue variety, as in "The Priority Line") are the object of frustration, if not torment. One begins to suspect "lines" is an unconscious leitmotif of the volume. In any event, both are first-rate poems, which are accompanied by other exemplary offerings in that particular genre.

These vivid creations remained with me for some time—a good measure of their efficacy as written art. To be sure, there are myriad other outstanding narratives contained in this bountiful volume, and all share the fine characteristics of the works cited. Without exception, they are deftly composed and emotionally compelling. It's no small feat to turn out a quality anthology on a yearly basis, and Nicholas has managed it no less than nine times. Kudos to him. In this so-called post-literate age, the world needs devotees of the word—publishers who provide a forum for creative expression and in so doing prevent the ageless art of story-telling from vanishing. It's been my honor and pleasure to appear in several issues of this per annum compilation (including this one), and it is my hope to do work that merits a place in future editions.

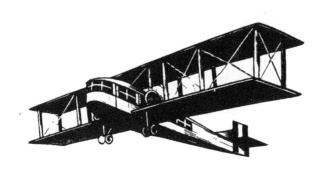

INTRODUCTION
Nicholas Litchfield

"A powerful literary passport—this adventurous anthology is all stamped up with exciting travel-themed writing. With humor, darkness, and charm, its lively prose and poetry will drop you into memorable physical and psychological landscapes."

— Joseph Scapellato, acclaimed author of Big Lonesome

Lowestoft Chronicle has been described in many intriguing and colorful ways. Iowa Short Fiction Award winner Ivy Goodman labeled it "a Baedeker for the vicarious traveler in the age of globalization." Reviewer Mary Beth Magee, of the news website Examiner.com, has described it as bringing "the far corners of the world to the reader's armchair," and author Scott Dominic Carpenter once called it "the literary equivalent of Rick's Café in *Casablanca*, where travelers of all stripes pull up a stool and swap stories at the bar."

Launched ten years ago, in the hope that it might survive for a few good years and, during that time, perhaps reach a happy, enviable spot amid the vast ocean of online literary journals all vying for room, it's the first and only literary magazine to come out of the coastal town of Lowestoft in Suffolk, England. At the time it set sail, I don't recall there being other online journals focused primarily on travel narratives and poetic wanderings.

Each year, we publish a "best of" collection as part of our mixed-form anthology series. Long-time *Lancashire Post* journalist Pam Norfolk noted that the previous one swept the reader to strange and exhilarating places and made them "yearn to strap on the backpack and go exploring," and bestselling novelist George Cockroft, who uses the pen name Luke Rhinehart, touted our first one as an impetus for inspiring him to want to write short stories again.

High praise indeed! Interestingly, Cockroft, best known for his 1971 cult classic novel *The Dice Man*, recently penned another critically acclaimed novel and is at work on a follow-up. Obviously, we don't pretend to have inspired him to put pen to paper again, but, hey, it's a nice thought!

As for *The Vicarious Traveler*, this marks our ninth little compendium of travel-inspired writings. Figuratively speaking, it's as inked up with entry stamp impressions as the passport of a continually on-duty air steward or a career diplomat for the Foreign Service. Crammed with thrilling adventures, thought-provoking travelogues, and stimulating poetry, we like to think of the book as a worldly, eye-opening souvenir for the recluse who has missed out on the wonders of globetrotting and, instead, left a substantial, enduring impression on the seat of his favored armchair.

In terms of geographical and psychological space, these poems, essays, and stories send the reader on a tumultuous voyage across the planet, taking in parts of Asia, Australasia, Africa, North America, and Europe. Robert Wexelblatt, a recipient of the Indie Book Awards first prize for fiction in 2008, put it more eloquently when he offered this description: "Here you will find journeys not only to varied locales in space and time but into the inexhaustible intricacies of human psychology, adventures of all sorts and in every genre." Although referring to one of our previous anthologies, I like to think that his statement applies to this collection, too. Indeed, there is a masterful, historical drama written by Wexelblatt himself in this anthology that matches that description. "Hsi-wei's Visit to Ko Qing-zhao," finds the Sui Dynasty vagabond poet Chen Hsi-wei, a likable character who has featured in many of Wexelblatt's stories, interfering in a court case in pursuit of justice while visiting his friend, an official in the magistrate's office.

Other far-flung adventures include "Alme," Michael C. Keith's gripping, mythical tale of a father and son, separated in a sandstorm in the Sahara Desert. Don Noel's "Monseigneur" is an intriguing account of his time in Phnom Penh in the mid-1960s, when he was under the constant watch of local police. There is "Turkish Apple Harvest," Dave Gregory's delightful tale of imprudent apple-picking, and "My Nephews and Nieces Will Boast with Pride," Michael Coolen's amusing memoir, in which he's schooled in the many harmful diseases he will likely contract while touring the Gambia as a Peace Corps Volunteer. There is also the riveting "The Treasure of Asō Lin" by M. T. Ingoldby, where two rival explorers journey across the world in the 1580s on an obsessive hunt for lost treasure, and Robert Perron's thrilling tour-de-force "Hippasus of Metapontum," where, on a stormy night off the coast of Greece, savage murder awaits a brilliant mathematician carrying a shocking and dangerous secret.

The ocean serves up further excitement in Rob Dinsmoor's scintillating apocalyptic tale, "Surf's Up!," and the creatures of the sea provide food for thought in Elaine Barnard's absorbing "The Jagalchi Fish Market," where a friendly founder rescues the day for a local fisherman at the world-famous South Korean fish market.

Elsewhere, solitary individuals find their inner tranquility tested by those around them. In Philip Barbara's engaging tale, "The Buzzing," a retiree's equilibrium is upset by an irksome neighbor's remote-controlled plane. In the stimulating "My Knee Had an Itch" by Richard Charles Schaefer, an independent woman on a solo vacation to Miami, content to be by herself, finds that the only lonely people are the ones who are not alone. On a sightseeing trip in Norway, the gregarious American helps thaw frosty relations between a quarrelsome British couple, in Mary Donaldson-Evans's witty "The Accidental Peacemaker." Matthew Menary provides a comic account of his first visit to France in "Oh, Pardon," as the altruistic American comes a cropper when he encounters a blind beggar in a busy métro station in Paris. And the unjust actions of an imperious hotel manager in Japan turn a well-mannered western businessman into a troublesome, iron-willed pest in Mark Halpern's droll "Life Is Grand."

The remaining story, "Armistice Day" by Dan Morey, is a sardonic tale of sibling rivalry. Full of barbed comments, playful jabs, and cutting retorts, the journey of two bickering brothers on a pilgrimage to France to honor their late father rapidly turns into an uninhibited slugfest.

Poetry forms an integral part of *Lowestoft Chronicle*, and, in keeping with the format of the magazine, it accounts for almost a third of the pieces here. Inspired either by distant memories of childhood, past relationships, significant journeys, remembered news stories, the pursuit of freedom and fresh surroundings, or new cultural experiences, these engaging works are primarily humorous, quietly reflective, and bristling with perspicacity.

In some of the poems, like Matthew Mitchell's nostalgic "Homesick," where a sports game stirs up poignant childhood memories for an Ohioan living in Texas, there is a strong feeling of displacement and a yearning to turn back the clock. In contrast, the narrator in Matt Mason's "You Turned Twenty-Five in EuroDisney," relates, with sober acceptance, a distant memory of a broken relationship that even the magic of Disney could not save.

In others, the poets cast a discerning eye on sea life, history, human nature, and those who fly their line and hook their catch either for a living or for sport. In Valerie Nieman's "Lovesick Walrus Turns Up on Orkney Beach," there is no joy for either the flippered marine mammal that braves the remote, harsh wilds of Scotland or for those who inhabit the northernmost island. Thomas Piekarski advises us, in "Ubiquitous," to not be submerged by our personal woes but to look all around us at the wonders of nature. In "Low Season in Grado," Gary Singh uses the enchanting power of a famous Venetian poet's words to guide him through the tranquil splendor of a historic seaside town located on a lagoon along Italy's northeast Adriatic coast. In "Trunyan," Douglas Cole offers up illuminating, passing impressions of an excursion through Indonesia, and as Joe Mills observes in his quietly meditative "Fishermen," the uninitiated, distant traveler may see much that is unfamiliar to him, but some things remain constant regardless of time or place.

Risks, challenges, and the potential for disaster are an inevitable part of the travel experience. Bold choices and deep plunges are considered in Diane G. Martin's marvelously expressive "Border Crossing." In the laugh-out-loud "Passport Control," Jean L. Kreiling vividly recollects the frenzied chaos at the Paris Charles de Gaulle Airport passport control area, and in James B. Nicola's breezy "Centerpieces at the Inn," twelve captivating jars of potpourri reflect the interesting characters that pass through the guesthouse lobby.

In some of the nonfiction pieces, the need to escape a stale existence and seek adventure outweighs the potential perils and inevitable hardship. In the wonderfully funny "One, Two, Three, Hike!" greenhorn hiker Lawrence Morgan bids farewell to merely reading about adventure and decides to brave the wilderness and conquer Arizona's demanding Rincon

Peak Trail, while romance blossoms and a marriage withers as globetrotting friends outstay their welcome in Italy in the upbeat "Touched by the Tuscan Sun" by Olga Pavlinova Olenich.

A couple of essays present fascinating reflections of childhood journeys back and forth along Route 66. Katie Frankel's "Miles of Asphalt" focuses on cherished memories of family vacations by car from Texas to California, while Sharon Frame Gay's "Song of the Highway" is a fiercely expressive depiction of life on the dusty highway.

In some of the more tongue-in-cheek pieces, David Macpherson provides observational and philosophical musings on airport boarding lanes in "The Priority Line." In "Noise," Brian James Lewis lets loose a humorous rant about in-car entertainment systems, and Joan Frank offers wry contemplations on the extravagant claims by authors professing to live in multiple faraway cities in "Location Sluts."

Included in this collection is "Mr. O'Brien's Last Soliloquy," a personal favorite of mine written by prize-winning micro fiction maestro Robert Garner McBrearty. In this deeply touching and life-affirming tale, a ninety-four-year-old man, reflecting on the events that marked his life, voices his sorrows, regrets, and offers pertinent advice. His gut-wrenching monologue serves as a life lesson: a reminder of the value of family and the importance of how we spend our time.

Fiction, poetry, and memoir aside, this anthology also includes interviews with crime writer Timothy J. Lockhart, author of two hardboiled suspense novels, and Matthew P. Mayo, a recent winner of the prestigious Spur Award and Wrangler Award. Here, Lockhart talks about his literary influences and his writing process, and Mayo discusses some of his favorite characters, as well as his multi-award-winning historical novel, *Stranded*.

To echo the sentiments of Mayo, who last year praised

"the ongoing wonders of *Lowestoft Chronicle*" for entertaining, enriching, and edifying armchair travelers and helping them "rove the globe without popping a sweat or breaking the bank," this year's compendium aims to deliver the reader into more diverse, varied, and enthralling situations than previously, yet not to the extent that one gets hopelessly lost and confused and headed for the drinks cabinet. As with series entries that have gone before, *The Vicarious Traveler* is expertly guided by a sublime huddle of littérateurs, all keen to wander the planet, embracing the unknown and revisiting distant memories from a new perspective. Perhaps almost like a reliable, well-stocked portmanteau, the book you now hold in your furrowed, inky fingers is the erstwhile traveling essential, catering for all one's many moods and whims and intellectual cravings.

So, bid the travel agent bon voyage, settle into the wide and welcoming arms of the restful armchair, and immerse yourself in these far-flung journeys and poetic travel enriched pages. Safe wanderings.

SURF'S UP!
Rob Dinsmoor

"Get in the car, Ashley! Now!" Dad yelled, and I didn't like the tone of his voice.

"I'm not going to North Conway! It's boring!"

"I don't care if you're bored! I care if you're still alive!"

He was being a drama queen, or at least that's what I thought at the time. I probably should have listened, but the whole climate change emergency thing happened so quickly. In just a few days, the winter temperature on the North Shore went from the 20s to the 80s, and for me, it was a dream come true. The first day it happened, my BFF Caitlin and I went to Singing Beach, along with half the population of Manchester. (That's Manchester, Massachusetts, by the way. The town was renamed "Manchester-By-the-Sea" so that people wouldn't confuse it with Manchester, New Hampshire. As if.)

There was still some snow toward the back of the beach, but it would be toast soon. We walked to the far end of the beach, where the rocks and the mansions are, slathered on some SPF15, and lay on our towels in our thong bikinis. There were plenty of guys playing football and Frisbee right next to us. Just a coincidence, right?

But then my parents started to panic. Dad said the temperature was supposed to hit 90 by the end of the week, but that there was really no telling because the meteorologists all said that the next several days were going to be totally unpredictable. "You may think you know what's going on, but trust me, you don't," he said. "There's no telling what kind of repercussions weather like this is going to have. We could have hurricanes, tornados, floods, you name it." Like I said, Dad was a real drama queen.

I remember one winter when I was in grade school, in 2007, when we had this freaky 70-degree day in February. It was totally awesome, but weird watching the sun set below the dunes at Crane Beach at 4:30 on a warm sunny day that felt like summer. I especially felt for the little kids playing with their shovels. For all they knew, it would stay warm and they would go to the beach every week—and they were in for a rude awakening. But the important thing was, there were no hurricanes and nobody died.

So, the last thing I wanted to do was get in the car with Mom, Dad, and Dakota and sit through traffic for hours to get to North Bumfuck, New Hampshire. I gave him the finger, climbed into my birthday Beamer, and took off. I decided to go see what Caitlin was up to.

Almost immediately, my cell phone rang, but I didn't pick up, letting it go straight to voicemail. When I pulled over, I listened to the voicemail. I expected him to ream me out, but this was even worse. "Ash, it's Dad. I'm sorry I was cross with you, but I'm very concerned. I hope you'll come join us up in North Conway. Please call us. I promise I'll be calmer when you call." Whatever.

Caitlin and I went back to Singing Beach, but nobody was there. That's probably because of the stench and the barricades. WTF? We got out of the car, walked across the parking lot and saw where the stink was coming from. There were a couple of whales that had washed up on the beach. It was gross, but also sad. I wondered whether they had been mates or something.

We drove up 127 to Magnolia Beach, which often stinks anyway because of all the mucky seaweed that hangs around at low tide, but today it stank even more than usual. At least one dead whale and what might at one time have been bluefish. We bagged it and went back to my house.

We watched TV while dining on ice cream and Mom's

white wine. Why not? If the world was going to end, we might as well enjoy our last moments, right? While channel-surfing, I came across an interview of some Harvard biologist talking about how accelerated global warming was affecting the eco-system, making wildlife migrate to places they didn't belong and generally behave in unexpected ways. He was followed by a meteorologist talking about a rapidly developing hole in the ozone layer over the East Coast. I switched channels and saw a clip about traffic on I-95. Absolutely horrendous. It was a parking lot, except that there were assholes driving way off the road to get ahead in the traffic.

"Gee, I wish I'd gone with my family up to North Conway!" I said.

"Really?" Caitlin asked. She can be really thick sometimes. "As if!"

After Caitlin left, I switched to *Game of Thrones*, available on demand, and fell asleep on the couch.

The next morning, I checked the surf report on my laptop and saw that, in the late afternoon, they were predicting a powerful offshore wind and four-foot waves on Good Harbor Beach—a perfect combination that doesn't come around very often. I've always considered Good Harbor to be a surf spot for newbies and other losers. But going to my favorite local spot, Hampton Beach, meant driving up I-95 or Route 1, which might even be worse. And, well, four-foot waves—that was something. I immediately called Caitlin, and she was game. Caitlin's parents were on vaca in Barcelona, so she could pretty much do what she wanted.

My surfboard was in the back of the garage, as I hadn't used it since, like, forever. Usually, I'd surf in my wetsuit up until early November, but then it got so cold I just couldn't stand it anymore, wetsuit or no. I looked out the window and saw some wild flowers and crocuses pushing up between patches of snow, along with butterflies! Sweet! But I had a nasty surprise when I opened the garage door.

It was full of spiders—huge and like none I'd ever seen—and they were literally covering everything in the garage with webs—rakes, hoes, shovels, the lawnmower, the snow blower, you name it. Don't get me wrong, I think spiders are really gross, but my love of surfing overrode my hatred for spiders. Never get between a girl and her longboard!

I went into the kitchen and came back with a lighter, the Sunday newspaper, and a broom. I rolled up the newspaper and lit the end of it so it made a lot of smoke. I put that on the floor of the garage and watched the spiders start to skitter away from it. Then I used the broom to break up the spider webs and clear a path to the surfboard. That's how I rescued it from the spider cave.

The trip to Caitlin's was uneventful, partly because there was practically no one on the road. The only obstacles were these stampeding hordes of chipmunks that kept running under my tires and getting squished. It was totally gross.

Caitlin came bounding out of her house as soon as I pulled up. She was dressed appropriately in a floral bathing suit and a baseball cap. We strapped her surfboard to the top of mine and headed for Good Harbor. All along the way, we caught occasional glimpses of the ocean, which was totally stirred up. The main entrance to the beach was closed, as it always was in the winter, so we parked on a side street and carried our boards down to the beach.

I was so happy to see that there were no dead whales, but the sand fleas were jumping—and biting. Not only that, but so were the greenheads, these nasty flies whose bodies are so hard you can't really crush them. The best thing you can do is smack them silly and then bury them in the sand, hoping they won't be able to wiggle their way out and bite you again. The weird thing is, I've seen them at Crane Beach but never Singing Beach, and certainly not in February.

The waves were epic. As we waded in with our boards, we noticed how warm the water was. Usually, at this time of year, it got down into the 50s, but this felt like one of those beaches on St. John, back before the hurricanes flattened it. At first, we were battered back by the waves, even though we tried to get under them and surface behind them.

On the right side, the rocks form a natural barrier. We paddled on our stomachs in between the rocks and shore and waited there until just after a wave had passed, shot out behind it, waited for another wave and, when it started to nudge our boards forward, stood up. We had a few glorious rides and were a little surprised no one else was out there.

It was after a few rides that I started to see those red patches forming on Caitlin's skin. Immediately, I looked down at my skin and I had them too!

"Caitlin!" I called out and she screamed, "Holy fuck, Ash! What's going on?"

"Maybe it's the ozone!"

"Let's get out of here!" she said, starting to paddle for shore. Then she called out "Holy--! Something just bit me!" She held out her right hand and there was blood on her fingers, but I couldn't tell how bad the bite was.

"What is it?" I cried out.

"I don't know! Something big!"

Caitlin started to paddle toward shore, but something violently tugged her arm and the water around her surfboard turned red. She held up what was left of her arm, screaming, and a few seconds later, a huge shark came out of the water and scooped her off the surfboard like a raw oyster.

As sometimes happens in an emergency, I took a moment to step back mentally from the situation. There was nothing I could do to save Caitlin at this point. Even though I was totally freaking out, I didn't paddle. Instead, I just crouched on the board until the waves washed me close to shore, into shallow water, jumped off, and sprinted onto the beach.

I ran back to the pile of stuff we'd laid out and put on my T-shirt and jacket to protect my skin, which was starting to blister and peel. Caitlin was nowhere to be seen.

I called 911 and the paramedics were there in 10 minutes. By then, the only signs of Caitlin were shreds of her floral bathing suit and some nondescript goo that the sand crabs got at immediately. The paramedics said there had been shark attacks all over Cape Ann. Apparently, something had gone wrong with their food supply, they said, and they were becoming particularly aggressive. They asked me all kinds of questions, including Caitlin's next of kin, and whether I wanted an ambulance or anything, but I declined. "You really should think about evacuating," one of them said.

"To where?" I asked, and he didn't have an answer.

I must have been numb with shock while they were there, but afterward, I'll admit it, I cried like a baby. I know it's lame, but that's what I did, remembering all the times Caitlin and I had growing up—boating, surfing, dating, and getting high. Then, for a while, I just sat there quietly, trying to think of nothing at all.

I checked my cell phone—I had a voicemail from Dad. "Hi, Pumpkin. Please call me. I'm afraid it's too late for you to drive up here. There have been out-of-control forest fires all over New Hampshire. It's complete chaos, and the police have barricaded the road because of violent episodes of road rage. Your Mom, Dakota, and I are holed up in the cabin with plenty of groceries, and I have my gas generator and rifle up here. I just wanted to hear your voice, in case I didn't have a chance anytime soon."

I continued to sit on that beach, contemplating things. The wind had picked up, blowing the sand around, and the waves were now huge, slamming against the rocks and even the mansion sitting on them. I remembered when Dad took me on a "photo expedition" during Hurricane Bill, back in 2009. Mom was bullshit, but Dad persisted, and we got lots of great photos and videos of huge waves crashing over the sea wall, and in some cases, slamming against mansions that had their windows all boarded up. Now, the sun began to set, turning the hemorrhaging clouds various shades of orange, pink and purple, as if someone had dropped food coloring into an aquarium and the crests of the waves and the mini sandstorms reflected all the pretty colors in the horizon.

I texted the picture to my Dad, adding, "I'm okay. It's a whole new world down here. Savage, but oh so pretty…"

FISHERMEN

Joe Mills

"Time is a river in which I go a fishing"
—Henry David Thoreau

In the downtown center of Tianjin,
among the skyscrapers and tour boats,
old men cast lines into the river
then sit on cushions, or makeshift chairs.
Around them, people walk, picnic, nap,
do forms, mind children, take selfies.
Throughout the day, the sun shifts
light and shadows across the water
as the fishermen watch and wait,
eating, exchanging cigarettes,
adjusting their poles and nets.
At dusk, they pack what they have
onto their bikes and mopeds,
and they go wherever it is men go
when they aren't sitting by a river.

Much about China is unfamiliar to me,
the language, food, signs, and traffic,
but not these men. I grew up with them.
Decades ago, in the American Midwest,
they were there on docks and river banks,
next to holes they had augured in the ice,
smoking, drinking, and telling stories
as the world around them shifted,
trees becoming houses becoming towers,
one century flowing into another.

THE JAGALCHI FISH MARKET
Elaine Barnard

It is late afternoon now, and still they haven't come, the tourists that I have been waiting for all day. Sometimes they come on buses, sometimes on foot, traveling from our myriad of subways that connect Busan from end to end. I myself love our subways, such an inexpensive mode of transport in South Korea, much better than cars because there is nowhere to park. That is, there is somewhere, but someone else has gotten there before you. So, you drive round and round in a daze with the other drivers honking you awake.

This day I have gotten to the Jagalchi Fish Market early as it is the weekend when the tides of tourists engulf us. My flounder and red snapper are in my tanks, submerged in the circulating waters that keep them fresh, ready for sale. They are beautiful to behold.

The tourists, when they finally come, will have many other options as well, crabs, eels, and the undulating tentacles of octopuses that I hear are delicious, almost like chicken. But I have never been able to eat an octopus since I discovered how smart they are. They are the stars of the Jagalchi Fish Market. My fish are not so smart, but I believe they are more beautiful. Just look at my snapper with her rosy skin and my flounder, his meat white and succulent, a gourmet's first choice.

I hear the din of the chopping blocks on the second floor where the fish is served. It is such a triumphant sound, *thud-thud-thud*. It blends with the chaos outside, the grind of the buses, the shrill calls of the grannies. The salty smell of fish and the pungent odor of frying oils delight me.

Soon, the grannies will slip on masks to filter the sewer smells, close up their food carts, and head home to prepare dinner for their working sons and daughters, to indulge the grandchildren with bits of their leftovers.

The sun, which has been bright all day, is setting. Shadows move along the aisles between the tanks. Many of the mongers have also left, as they've sold most of their fish to Jackie's restaurant upstairs, or to the housewives who purchase the crabs or eels for tonight's supper. They will steam or grill them simply with lemon so that you taste the delicious flavor of the fish, or dip them in chili and soy sauce if they are not so fresh.

The rubber boots that I have been wearing all day to slosh through the wet floors are beginning to be uncomfortable. I feel my feet swelling inside them as if my circulation has ceased. Also, my hands within these long rubber gloves are almost numb. I long to go home, to sit in a tub of hot water with my wife, to drink soju and make the night happy. I try to do this always, to make the night happy, but my wife disapproves. "The soju will be your undoing," she says. But I do not care. I love soju, so sweet and smooth. It trickles down my throat, warming my stomach, my legs, and hands, which are cold from sloshing in the waters all day, making sure my fish are fresh. They are my true loves. I watch them play in the waters. I hate to sell them, but I must. My wife says I love my fish more than her. She is probably right, but I will never admit it. How long would our marriage last if I did?

My wife works here too. She prints our cards, which she distributes to the tourists, hoping they will buy our fish instead of another monger's and bring the fish upstairs to Jackie's, where it will be prepared for a sumptuous meal.

My wife is getting tired of her work. She is not so pretty anymore. It is more difficult to lure the tourists who prefer younger faces that have been botoxed in the clinics or had a double fold added to their eyelids to make them look bigger, more Western. My wife would love to have her eyelids done. I tell her as soon as we have the money she can have all the surgeries she wants. But that day has never come and maybe never will. So, she has to be content with the face God gave her, the face I fell in love with and still do adore, next to my fish, which seem to have captured the larger part of my heart.

My wife waves to me from across the market, signaling it's time to close up, even though I have sold no fish today. Her black hair is limp from the moisture rolling in from the ocean which fronts the Jagalchi Fish Market. The gray in her roots is more prominent now, even though she uses the black dye sold in the markets. It is pitiful for women to age. They depend so much on their beauty to overcome life's difficulties.

If she wishes to go home, I must as well. It's not that I don't want to sit in the tub with her, but our earnings are meager, and this day will make them more so. I hate to leave my fish alone at night, even though I will leave the waters circulating to keep them fresh. I will worry about them all evening, dream of their safety, knowing they will long for my return in the morning, my sweet snapper and my favorite flounder.

Suddenly, I smell the fumes of a bus pulling up outside. I hear the laughter and the voices, jubilant from the day's outing. I hope they're still hungry, even though they probably had a big lunch. The students hustle inside, their elderly professor explaining the signs which are all in Korean. They mumble to each other in English, which I find difficult to understand. There is no music to their syllables.

They are with the octopus now. Their professor extolls the wonders of its tentacles, how it can capture its prey, then raves about the black ink of the squid, how it is a staple of the gourmet's diet. His students poke each other and giggle, imitating the tentacles of the octopus, spitting the black ink of the squid.

I am waiting for them to pass my tanks. I stand at attention, a smile on my face. It is my best smile – the one I use for the tourists. My wife is also smiling, her cards ready to distribute, to tell the tourists about her discount if they will buy our fish and send it upstairs to Jackie's to be prepared for a late lunch or early dinner. But they are paying no attention to my tanks, to my elegant snapper or favorite flounder. They are enraptured by the octopus. I smile wider, hoping the flash of gold in my teeth might attract them for a second, get them to pause before they leave.

"Where is the restroom?" a skinny girl pleads, shifting her backpack. The professor squints at the signs, then points her in my direction. She must pass my tanks to get there. Just as she passes, my favorite flounder jumps from the tank, hitting the patched thigh of her jeans. I rush with my net to scoop him back into the water. She looks dumbfounded. "Oh, how sweet," she coos. "Look at it, everyone."

They gather around her, staring, chuckling, debating what they should do with my friendly flounder. "Let's send him upstairs to Jackie's," they chorus. "He'll make a great dinner."

"Yeah, he's huge enough for all of us," another kid yells.

"No," the girl interrupts as he wiggles in my net. "I'm a vegetarian. Let's take him to the docks. We can send him back where he came from." She pulls out some won from her pack. "Is this enough?" she rolls the bills in her sweaty palm, her blue eyes hopeful.

I'm not sure it is. I feel a pang in my heart, my favorite flounder gone back to the sea. I hesitate, but my wife intercedes. "It is enough," she snaps, sealing the flounder in a baggie of water. "But hurry, before my husband changes his mind."

TRUNYAN
Douglas Cole

Children swim in the waters
around the dock.
We move through the village
of meager homes, dirt streets,
to the temple.
Someone has placed money
on the temple steps.
This is how much to enter.
I slip some rupiah
under the stone that holds the money.
Inside, our guide translates
the story of Ratu Gede Pusering Jagart,
the sacred stone that appears
on the night of
Purmamaning Sasih Kapat.
No earthquake has ever hit
this village, one man tells us.
In another shrine
they have a lontar,
the sacred manuscript of the village,
carved into a root, so old
the language is like nothing
that exists—a story
no one can read.
And then the graveyard:
the dead lie above the ground
beneath a row of skulls.

They have little whicker tents
for covering...
yellow umbrellas, bits of cloth,
a brass bowl for offerings.
On the slope below the graves,
a heap of remains: bones, clothing,
more skulls and rotting whicker
from the old graves.
Our guide draws on a clove cigarette,
smoke barely covering
the smell of decaying flesh.
We didn't ask to come,
and he's impatient for his money.

THE TREASURE OF ASŌ LIN
M.T. Ingoldby

Legend has it that when the proud and ruthless wokou Asō Lin perished on the deck of the *Takanobo*, she left her considerable spoils buried on an island only she could locate. Her last words taunted her crew: They could take her life but would gain nothing by it. Her fortune would forever be her own.

The outline is brief since our story begins almost fifty years later when the rumor of Asō Lin's treasure first reached the shores of England. Such a rumor could hardly fail to excite the public, whose fascination with piracy is echoed by much of the era's fiction, but its impact on the lives of two men, Ben Monke and Lord McNay, and the curious fates it entailed for both, are as worthy of our interest as the pirate queen herself.

By no means were Monke and McNay the only expeditors of their era. In the wake of Raleigh and Drake, any man with the capital to charter a ship and a crew would invariably cast their fortunes to sea. A fair number never came back. Many more proved slightly successful; here and there a new taste, expression, tool or garment made its way into Elizabethan culture. However, Monke and McNay were known less as pioneers than for their longstanding public rivalry. As is often true of two people with similarly oriented egos, they held each other in extreme contempt; which, sadly, reached new heights after two recent voyages almost brought them both to ruin.

The first of these was Monke's who, in May of 1580, sailed out from Bristol to prolong the setting of the sun. Benedict Monke was a short, brusque-mannered heir to minor aristocracy. He had no difficulty in obtaining a ship. However, owing to a crisis of navigation, his crew traveled less than a thousand nautical miles to Iceland; which, this being one of very few voyages the crew had actually made, they mistook for the New World. After a further eight months at sea, they returned to England with a cargo of a noisome herb that did not find a market and is not used today. It is said that in frustration, Monke ordered the entire boatload be tossed into the sea.

More or less concurrently, Lord McNay ('Lord' being his middle name, adopted as his first) returned from many months of eastward exploration with thirty-three crates of gray powder, to be chewed to a paste, then expectorated in the custom (or so he was led to believe) of the Arawak tribe in what we now call Suriname. Unlike tobacco, as popular then as today, the internal damage caused by *arasin* was quickly apparent, superficially by a blackening of the nostrils and lips. McNay paid by reputation: He had the misfortune to be regarded as both imbecile and thwarted mass-murderer. Such was his pride, however, that he continued to stain his own sinuses until he died.

Both failures put pressure on each of them to restore their good names, and all the talk of Asō Lin in the dockland set Monke thinking. On June 16th, 1581, he issued a public challenge in the *Evening Standard*: Any man who saw fit to call himself a captain is hereby warned, G. B. Monke intends to claim the treasure of Asō Lin—or forfeit his ship to the person who does. No-one doubted whom the challenge was intended for, and sure enough, two days later, a curt response appeared on the same page:

Your ship you may keep. The treasure is mine. Sincerely, L. McNay.

Monke had good reason to throw down this particular gauntlet. Not a week before, an associate of his had covertly obtained the complete recovered diaries of Asō Lin, in which the location of a secret map was said to be disclosed. The purchase nearly bankrupted the luckless explorer, but the rewards hinted at were more than worth it; of the two, he had most to gain by the wager, and he was confident of his advantage.

As Monke foresaw, his ash-mouthed rival (who of the two was more inclined to reckon on his luck) took a very different approach.

As the scourge of the Philippine Sea, Asō Lin would undoubtedly have found an island for her bounty there. And so, lacking perhaps an accurate perception of that ocean's size, McNay chartered a ship and a crew and set sail from Plymouth a mere three weeks after the challenge was made.

Acting on the hint of an unmapped outcrop off the coast of Papua New Guinea, McNay was also confident of his advantage, seemingly upheld by a steady wind that accompanied them down the coast of Africa. The Cape of Good Hope would curtail this run of fortune—but for now, let us leave them in high spirits, bawling sea ballads and facing manfully into the wind.

———— ✦ ————

The diary of Asō Lin was a heavy tome—malodorous and concerned as much with reporting the weather as with details of real piracy. The sacking of the Rumi coast earned a mere three lines, while the flight paths of black-bellied terns occupied over six pages. Nonetheless, Monke devoured the whole tome with even diligence, turning the brittle pages with his winter gloves.

After several months, he discovered only two mentions of a map—at least, those that weren't expunged by ocean spray. The first confirmed the drawing of one on April 2nd, 1518, while berthed in Mangalore. The second boasted of an intricate code that would prevent the chance acquirer from interpreting it— knowledge of which entailed access to both an aviation map and a compass.

The deeper he dove, the more the diary seemed to demand of him. Cipher piled on cipher, code upon code until Monke had crowded countless pages of his own with calculations, ink tests, alphabets, alien symbols, and spidery annotations—all without absenting his study (which he locked at all times), or the reference rooms of the British Library.

In abject contrast, McNay's crew were now freezing, exhausted, and lost in the extreme—somewhere in the Bay of Bengal. By secret consent, the sky and ocean deemed them far enough from land to bully without mercy: The mainsail tore, became two white flags; lightning danced on the horizon; then the vessel was gripped by a whirlpool and only just released, though not without loss of life and vital navigational equipment. Storms waylaid them, sheering paint from the hull until their maps were useless even as kindling. Both masts toppled in submission, and then they were discarded in a sudden calm.

The superstitious crew believed the ship was cursed. They mutinied, roping three life rafts together and seizing every scrap of food for their escape. Two of them were picked up by fishermen near Itu Aba and made new lives with the settlers from Hainan, building huts for themselves a considerable distance from the shore.

———— ✦ ————

To Ben Monke—still ensconced in London—the wokou's diary held no less turmoil than the oceans it described. He was by now educated in both Spanish and crude Japanese; he could chart the meteorology of seas he'd never visited, at times he'd never lived, and knew a porpoise from a narwhal, a junk from a caravel, without having seen any of them. His mind was awash with the deeds of Black Bellamy and Shirahama Kenki in such detail as would chasten a scholar.

Nights and days were negated by endless research. More than once he leaped up from his chair, convinced that someone had been spying over his shoulder. Accordingly, all servants were dismissed, and guests were discouraged from returning. His work would not be interrupted.

And yet, the more he unraveled, the more paranoid he became that he'd missed something; that while he slept, or tried to, his rival had chanced upon the hidden trove; that the riddle was endless; that some other anxiety kept him rooted to England. He talked under his breath of spies, traps, cryptograms, and opportunists waiting to swoop down and appropriate his work. When the puzzle seemed to demand a grasp of Portuguese, he chose to study it himself rather than entrust the translation to a stranger. In the same way, where Asō Lin had computed her crew's wages, he saw yet another code, one that might elucidate a pattern in the dates that so far had proved unyielding.

There was a thread. Sometimes it appeared that way, in dreams, a silvery ribbon like moonlight on the water that scattered the moment he reached for it. There were clues, but far too many. Likely spots included Pulau Nias, the Nicobar Islands, or somewhere in the Sulu Sea. However, setting out to any of them would leave the others exposed to Lord McNay, who might be there already. The indecision shucked his fingernails and locked his face into a lasting wince.

By luck, a few kind peers intervened. At first, Monke dispatched them. Later, he confided in them that he was secretly adrift and afraid. His mind was not his own. They counseled him.

At last, to a shame that he would never overcome, his search was over. For the sake of his health, he had failed. He could only pray the loot stayed lost—his sanity depended on it.

———— ✦ ————

At that moment, or so it is cleaner to assume, McNay awoke to a sky made of rock. He could not feel the wind. A drop of seawater on his cheek roused him to further inspection: It seemed the leaking hull had found refuge in a cave. He could hear the ocean distantly; the cave was very long and echoed.

As if in a dream, McNay lifted himself from the deck and staggered into darkness, finding new strength with every step, though the wet sand desired his knees. The way led upwards, through many pitch-black contortions, the walls of which started to feel like earth. He was spilled at last into a bulb-shaped chamber; groping there, his hand met wood.

He pulled. A chest emerged from the sand, unremarkable in all but location. Now, his hands pried at the lid, knowing full well its contents would, like him, never leave the cave. There inside was a single piece of paper.

Numbly, he unfolded it. Drawn in the same hand that Monke would attest to be Asō Lin's own was a map, but of no lines he recognized, no coast he knew, and with no key he could decrypt. After a time, he laughed and tore it into pieces, then, suddenly exhausted, settled down for his final prayer.

---------- ✦ ----------

And now we must make a voyage of our own, possible only by proxy, through thirty years….and find the contest long forgotten, save by one man: Ernest Monke, in whose heart timorous unhappiness has festered. Though free of his burden, the captain made no effort to resume his former life; instead, his malaise took the form of a chronic restlessness, as though dogged by a slow-moving menace he could only temporarily delay.

Soon after closing the diary for good, he sold his flat in London for another outside Inverness, where he left no impression before moving again, this time abroad to Kungshamn, a Swedish coastal town. Several fishermen there were glad of his help, but most hadn't caught his name. He had an old book, they said, which never left his side; a bible, so they thought. On Monke ventured, bearing east, settling briefly in

Khadjibey (now called Odessa) and Muscat, by the Gulf of Oman. Next, he was spotted in Sri Lanka.

Only at night, in the voyages of sleep, did Asō Lin still disturb him, speaking passages she knew by heart, and telling him not to despair, since her fortune was never his, or anyone's, to find. He died on August 4th, 1593. Perhaps by then, he believed it.

———— ✦ ————

Monke's last years were spent in a little bungalow perched with almost comical precarity atop the desolate gray ridge of the Kagoshima coast. His only neighbor operated a lighthouse that was mostly obscured behind the fog. He was discovered many weeks after his death.

What effect this had, if any, on the final event of our tale was not in any case immediate. Almost half a century would pass before the gradual erosion of the tide (which none can truly escape) exposed a great fissure in the cliff just below the lighthouse, where a stockpile of gold coins, weapons and jewelry was at last revealed.

What had drawn Monke toward it is a mystery; not even he could have guessed the true pull on his compass. As it happened, the discovery of Asō Lin's fortune is owed entirely to the East China Sea.

So, too, is the return of McNay's ship in 1607, delivered to the shallows of Bougainville Island. McNay alone was found, a near-skeleton caught in the rigging. Of his former crew, we may assume the worst.

Today, fragments of Asō Lin's treasure are displayed in the British Museum, the Zhejiang Provincial Museum, and the Rekihaku in Chiba, Japan.

MONSEIGNEUR
Don Noel

A high-pitched voice, apparently amplified by radio, filled the evening air as my *cyclo-pousse* driver pedaled slowly through residential streets of Phnom Penh. The voice faded as we left that block, but reverberated in the next block, and the next.

"*Qui ça?*" I asked in my rusty French, looking over my shoulder. Who could that be?

He leaned down. "*C'est Monseigneur.*"

Of course! Norodom Sihanouk. Prince and then King Sihanouk, strictly speaking, but he had a few years earlier abdicated (in favor of his father) and had a constituent assembly create a constitutional monarchy, making him its first prime minister. By the time I arrived, he had decided to be head of state. But no one called him by any of those titles: In Khmer he was *Samdech*, but for Cambodians with any command of French he was universally spoken of (and to) as *Monseigneur*.

As my introductory tour of Phnom Penh continued, we were never entirely out of reach of that piercing voice. "*Toute le monde écoute?*" I asked. Did everyone in the whole damned city tune in when Sihanouk took to the radio?

"*Oui, certainement,*" my driver answered.

I would in time learn that he often spoke for an hour or more, exhorting his people or his National Assembly to build a better nation, offering health tips, on one occasion even reading a long Israeli tract on how to promote tourism. Each declamation, a radio official would tell me, was re-broadcast at least once, and—if it was important—twice. He couldn't remember any speech that had been deemed unimportant.

It was my second evening in Cambodia, in September of 1966. I had arrived and initially checked into a downtown Chinese-run hotel—*hôtel commerçant*—suggested by the friend who had made my coming possible. I'd just begun unpacking when the room door opened and a woman, not young but well endowed, barged in. She asked—I was too flustered to remember how she put it—whether I wanted her services. When I said "No, *merçi*," she smiled and left, murmuring something like "maybe later."

I spent the night there – being sure the door was locked—but looked around the next morning, and discovered that the Hotel Le Royal, the country's premier accommodation, had attic "student rooms," not air-conditioned, that were within my budget. I signed up and headed back downtown for my suitcase. There were only occasionally taxicabs lined up outside the hotel awaiting fares, but there were always several *cyclo-pousses*, the most common form of hired transportation. I took the first one who pedaled up to the door and had him wait at the downtown hotel while I collected my stuff and checked out.

When I stepped out that evening, the same man hurried to the Hôtel le Royale door to offer his services. I managed to convey that I just wanted to cycle through the city to get a sense of it. (My freshman-college French was stilted and halting in the first few weeks, but by the time I left Cambodia five months later I was tolerably proficient.)

The cyclo-pousse was a bicycle whose front end was a two-wheeled cart, with a seat wide enough for two, passengers' feet as exposed as bumpers. Most of them had a plastic roof and front closure that could be deployed (not unlike an American convertible, but not nearly so sophisticated) to keep passengers reasonably dry—but not the men pedaling behind.

This was a balmy, dry evening. A few blocks from the hotel, my driver leaned over my shoulder: Would I like him to find me a Chinese woman?

I shook my head. He pedaled on a few yards, and leaned in again: A Vietnamese woman?

I shook him off again, but he persisted. A Cambodian woman? Amused that this was so obviously a third-choice option, but beginning to be annoyed, I shook my head decisively.

He pedaled on in silence—we had not yet reached the residential blocks where *Monseigneur* was holding forth—and leaned in once more: Would I like a boy?

If nothing else, my first two days told me that many of the foreigners who came to Cambodia, for whatever other reason, must welcome the pleasures of the flesh.

Not, by the way, American visitors. I was at the moment the only American in the country. Sihanouk, annoyed by the way the Vietnam War slopped over the border from time to time, had broken off diplomatic relations some 16 months before my arrival. (He also, I would learn, hoped to assuage the parliamentary left-wingers who called themselves the Khmer Rouge. Only after Sihanouk was deposed did the Cambodian Reds abandon parliamentary changes to begin their rampage and killing fields.)

I was an Alicia Patterson Fellow, to spend half a year in Cambodia and the second half in Romania. My principal assignment was exploring the impact of current politics versus centuries-old animosities in determining how decisions were made in governing and developing major rivers (the Mekong and the Danube) when the riparians were ideological adversaries.

I won a visa with the help of a Quaker pacifist friend who had recently run an international seminar in Cambodia, who volunteered to write on my behalf. On my third day, I *cycloed* (with the same man pedaling) across the city to Sihanouk's offices. His personal aide, a young man with excellent English, suggested I come back with a formal letter outlining all the agencies and places I wanted to visit.

I did so, delivering it the next day, and then spent a nervous two days waiting for an answer. Finally, I was called back, and the aide handed back my letter. Beside each item I had listed was hand-written "*D'accord*"—okay. At the foot of the letter was a huge N for Norodom.

"What do I do with this?" I asked.

"Show it to anyone you want to visit or interview," he said.

My first test of that, by pure serendipity, came a few days later. I took a boat upriver to Kompong Chom, where I had arranged to tour an agricultural cooperative the next day. Arriving early, I checked in to a little hotel, then went for a walk. There were still children in school a few blocks away; I paused to take a few notes and was accosted by a security officer who asked me to come explain myself to the principal.

I told the gentleman, in my still-limping French, about my fellowship studies. Did I have any documentation? he asked. Well, I said tentatively, I have this letter, although it doesn't mention your school. I handed it over.

His eyes widened. "*C'est l'écriture de Monseigneur!*" He had somehow recognized Sihanouk's handwriting, probably that Napoleonic N. He spent the next hour telling me all about his school and Cambodian education.

That letter became my passport. I took it everywhere, in a stiff envelope, but by the time I left it was worn and tattered.

Although *Monseigneur* made sure I could go wherever I wanted, I began to suspect that he or his police were keeping careful track of my wants. My cyclo-pousse driver of that first evening seemed almost always available; in my five months in Phnom Penh, there were only two others who occasionally filled in. None of the three would give me a name; my notes record them only by the number of the license plate appended to the back of the bicycle.

In my second month, I arranged a trip to study health facilities and more farm cooperatives in the western town of Battambang, close enough to Siem Reap that I decided to take a couple of leisure days to visit Angkor Wat. Much of that vast millennium-old complex was still being painstakingly pried from the jungle grasp and reconstructed, mostly under the guidance of French archaeologists. I checked into a pleasantly French-tropical hotel in the late morning and spent the rest of the day touring the temples.

The hotel had an outdoor garden restaurant, and after a quick shower I went out to order dinner and catch up notes. I'd barely gotten started when a well-dressed Cambodian came to my table. Was I alone? Might he join me? Of course, I said, glad for a chance to pick his brains.

The picking was quickly reversed. He sat down, ordered dinner, and initiated a conversation about how my day had gone. He seemed interested in every detail; the thought grew on me that his visit was not casual. The conversation was in French, and I was struggling, but I managed to find the words to ask, "You're supposed to report on me, aren't you?"

To my surprise, he confessed readily. He should have been here the night before, but he had a domestic crisis and missed the train. He hoped I would understand, and help him out.

I not only finished a detailed account of my first day but made a bargain with him: If he would forgo any clumsy efforts to shadow me—and enjoy, himself, a visit to the temples—I would meet him here for dinner each evening and give him a detailed accounting of my day. He must have decided I was an honest man and not a subversive: He agreed.

We both kept our sides of the bargain: I didn't see him anywhere on each of my next two days' wanderings, and I gave him an exhaustive accounting at dinner each evening. I had no way to tell, but I suspected that he would win praise and perhaps even promotion, back in Phnom Penh, for the thoroughness of his surveillance.

On the last two days of my stay in Cambodia, I engaged each of my three *cyclo-pousse* drivers to take me, one at a time, out on long trips into the countryside. I had each stop at a bucolic spot far from houses or villages, places we would not be seen or heard. I thanked each for his service, proffered a substantial tip, and—assuring them that I would soon be gone, so there could be no repercussions for honesty—asked each: Whom do you report to?

The police, each of the three said. Once a week, while a policeman took notes, each recited where I'd gone, how long I'd stayed, who if anyone had come out to see me off, how pleased I'd seemed on the way back to the hotel. One admitted receiving a modest fee for his reporting. The other two denied they'd been compensated for their surveillance but explained that the police might give them traffic tickets or even suspend their *cyclo-pousse* licenses if they failed to cooperate.

I was not surprised; since the friendly interviews with my Angkor Wat shadow, there had been other indications that I was under careful watch.

It wasn't only the voice of *Monseigneur* that was omnipresent; his eye was on me, too.

HIPPASUS OF METAPONTUM
Robert Perron

The ship's ladder swayed left and right, along with the contents of my stomach, forcing a frantic clamber from the center hold with no time to admire the hazy half-moon over the bow. I grasped the port-side rail as we surged uphill at the incline of a three-four-five triangle, teetered on wave's crest, and plummeted at the same pitch. Except for last night's supper, which rose and spewed over the rail into the white-capped brine.

"Aye," said a voice beside me. "Let her all out. You'll feel the better for it."

Out it gushed, mutton and wine, followed by a dry retch. I pulled the sleeve of my tunic across my mouth and looked to the source of the nocturnal wisdom, a wide face of white stubble beneath a bald pate. His frame resembled a barrel set on two staves. He wore nothing but a sleeveless, white chiton [kiton] against the night draft, and stood upon the galloping deck as I would Mother Earth on a calm afternoon.

"My advice, sir," he said, "take some air before retiring. It'll settle ye stomach and steady ye legs."

The ship fluttered on another crest, and my fingernails cleaved the rail as we dove for the wave's trough. My companion smiled, planted to the deck as steady as the mast behind him.

"And I would welcome a chat," he said, "to break the monotony of the watch."

"If you please," I said, "whom am I addressing?"

"Orestes the mariner, ye are, my young sir, sometimes called Orestes the ancient mariner."

"What's your age, then, ancient one?"

"Not a clue, sir, but I've been asea longer than anyone I

know, including Kastor, the master of this boat."

My stomach calmed, as did the ship, not soaring and diving as before, or perhaps my imagination and sickness had exaggerated the turbulence. I removed one hand from the rail and straightened my posture.

"Now, good sir," said Orestes, "tell me, what is this distinguished group we convey to Miletus [myleetus]? Are ye mathematicians?"

"We're mathematicians and philosophers," I said. Then added sotto voce [sado voce], "Followers of Him."

"Ah," said the ancient mariner, "Pythagoreans."

"Indeed," I said, surprised that a simple sailor possessed knowledge beyond the myths of the sea. "We're on our way to a conference."

"And which of your greybeards is the illustrious Philolaus [Filolayus]? He must be the oldest and loudest, the one with the curly-haired lad in tow."

Again, a surprise. That an ordinary seaman knew the name of a philosopher, albeit one of renown. However, he'd erred regarding identity.

"No," I said, "that's not Philolaus. The one with the lad is Hippasus."

"Of course," said Orestes. "I've heard of him, too. A contemporary of the great man, of Him himself, am I right?"

"You're correct." What an extraordinary fellow, I thought—knowledgeable, inquisitive.

"And the lad?" said Orestes.

"The lad is Demetrios, assistant and ward to Hippasus."

Orestes clapped his hands. "Aye, we should all have the assistance of such ruddy cheeks." He extended an elbow as if to nudge me. "And I don't mean the ones upon his face." I indulged his coarse humor with a chuckle.

"If it's Philolaus you're looking for," I said, "think of the most reserved, the sternest person aboard."

"Ah, I know the one you mean. Who can miss him?"

"He represents the predominant view despite Hippasus's seniority."

"Do they get along," said Orestes, "Hippasus and Philolaus?"

I moved my face close to the mariner's toothless countenance. "Not at all," I said. "Philolaus considers Hippasus a heretic."

Orestes raised an eyebrow. "How so?"

"Hippasus doubts the harmonics of numbers. He says there exist numbers that are not true ratios."

Orestes rubbed his chin as though considering the suggested abstraction. "Aye, but suppose there are such numbers?"

I took a half step back, releasing my grip on the rail and losing my balance. Orestes threw out a forearm which I clutched.

"No disrespect meant, sir. I'm just saying—is there any way to decide the issue?"

Again, I leaned into the sailor's sagging face. "Tomorrow at noon Hippasus is making a presentation. We're putting up a sandbox amidship, weather permitting."

"It should be a fine day, sir. This bit of roughness will pass."

———— ✦ ————

Next day, on a calm sea, as Helios's chariot approached its zenith, Demetrios, wearing a light blue citron [kiton] with gold trim, and no undergarments, raked the sandbox smooth. A semicircle of thirty Pythagoreans watched, Philolaus at one edge, arms crossed, Hippasus in the center. My perch lay midway in the second rank, where I craned my neck, edged out by the greybeards. I felt an elbow in my left rib cage and glanced to my side to see Orestes.

"You take an interest in mathematics?" I said.

"Aye, sir, and astronomy. It keeps us afloat."

Hippasus stepped forward, turned, and faced us, tall body with an angular face and slanted smile, contemporary of the great man, Him himself. "We seek the truth," he said. "Do we not?"

I looked to Philolaus for a hint of a reaction, but he was wont to give emotive displays.

"Yes, yes," said the Pythagoreans, "get on with it."

Hippasus turned to Demetrios and said, "Would you be so kind as to draw two lines, one perpendicular upon the other?"

The boy placed a stick with a cord in the sand, stretched the cord, and snapped it to create a line. He attached a second stick, drew arcs, aligned the cord on their vertices, and snapped a perpendicular.

"Well done," said Hippasus. "Now mark off ten equal measures on each line."

Demetrios shortened the length of cord between the two sticks and bent to the task.

"A fine lad," whispered Orestes.

"Now," said Hippasus, "connect the ends to form a triangle."

I bent sideways toward Orestes. "Are you following this?"

"Aye, sir, he's making a right isosceles triangle with the legs measuring ten units each."

Hippasus raised a finger and his voice. "Do we agree that the area of each leg of this triangle comprises a hundred squares? And that the hypotenuse—" Hippasus pointed to the last line snapped by Demetrios. "And that therefore the hypotenuse is the root of two hundred squares."

"Yes, yes," said the greybeards.

"But what is the precise value?" said Hippasus. "Demetrios, mark off the hypotenuse using the same measure as for the legs."

Swinging the two sticks, Demetrios marked fourteen measures along the hypotenuse, the last falling just short of the end. The boy swung again, and the fifteenth mark fell beyond the end of the hypotenuse. A murmur swept along the semicircle, more of dismay than surprise, for the problem was known, if not the solution.

"Clearly," said Hippasus, "the hypotenuse cannot be apportioned in terms of the legs."

"Come, come," said a greybeard. "You just haven't found the measure."

"I've tried every number to ninety-six, with great care, on large plots of sand. Nothing comes out. As the measure grows smaller, the line approaches a harmonic. But it's obvious that it will never get there." Hippasus pointed into the sandbox. "The hypotenuse of this triangle is immeasurable."

"Impossible," said a greybeard.

"Absurd," said another.

Philolaus unfolded his arms and stepped into the sandbox. He lacked the height of Hippasus and his sonorous delivery, but eyes of coal shriveled the strongest heart. He ground a sandal in the center of the hypotenuse, looked first at Hippasus, then the rest of us.

"This is not a proof," he said.

"Of course it's not a proof," said Hippasus. "It's a demonstration so even the densest among us can understand the issue. Even that bowlegged gaffer."

For an instant, I thought Hippasus was pointing at me, my loins puckering until I realized he meant Orestes, who said, "Aye, sir, and I take your meaning."

Laughter rippled from the Pythagoreans except for Philolaus.

"There is a proof," said Hippasus. "A proof by contradiction which I intend to present at the conference." He cast a finger at the trodden hypotenuse. "I will show beyond doubt that this line is immeasurable."

A gasp arose, more for the tone of Hippasus's remarks than their substance. Although the substance was, in fact, the problem.

"Your so-called proof is not on the syllabus," said Philolaus.

"What are you afraid of?" said Hippasus.

———— ✦ ————

Night passed without incident, neither the sea nor my stomach churning. I was making a breakfast of flatbread, goat cheese, and grapes when yells and thumps assailed the center hold from the adjacent greybeards' cabin. A scream, the voice of Hippasus, then muffled echoes.

We looked around, us lesser philosophers, but made no move. It was not for us to dispute the actions of our begetters. We heard grunts rising toward the deck and took our own ladder into a post-dawn mist on an undulating deck. Eight greybeards stood about a squirming mass the length and breadth of Hippasus, wrapped in two cloaks, tied with cord top, middle, and bottom. There must have been a rag stuffed in his mouth for he emitted only inarticulate gobbles.

Two greybeards swayed across the deck and staggered back under the weight of a bag of sand gripped between them. They plopped it midway on the squirming sack of Hippasus and secured it with another cord.

I backed away from the proceedings and saw Orestes standing amidst his shipmates. He walked my way. I said, "They're just trying to scare him."

"I fear you're wrong, sir. They mean to drown him."

I edged closer to ensure our privacy. "But he had a mock court if any. These actions are akin to murder."

"Not," said Orestes, "if the master of the boat agrees."

I looked to the helm where Kastor stood, legs apart, arms crossed, thick black hair rippling in the wind, eyes above the fray.

"How could he agree to such an extremity?" I said.

"Scuttlebutt has it he's been promised the curly-haired lad for the duration of the voyage."

I looked to Orestes for a sign of disgust or distress, but

his demeanor appeared whimsical as he gazed west. I looked again to the master of the ship, then back to the commotion upon the deck. The greybeards, four to a side, were dragging Hippasus to the port-side rail.

I said to Orestes, "Did you understand the demonstration yesterday? The immeasurability of the hypotenuse?"

"Aye."

"Doesn't he make sense? Isn't he on to the truth?"

At the port-side rail, sixteen hands grasped and lifted.

"Heave," said Philolaus.

The wriggling cloaks, corded and sandbagged, held the sea's surface for a pulse beat then sank. For a second pulse beat, the sack remained visible in the blue-green Aegean then faded beneath the ripples. Philolaus and the greybeards turned and marched away as having disposed of a dog gone mad.

"Aye, the truth," said Orestes.

Of a sudden, the deck surged from port to starboard, and back. Whitecaps appeared on cresting waves.

"Poseidon is angry," I said.

"Nonsense, sir," said Orestes. "Ye don't believe those fairy tales, do ye?" He pointed west. "This storm's been in the making since afore dawn. But look at ye, sir."

I stared into Orestes's countenance to catch his meaning as wind and sea roiled the ship under scattered droplets. The deck had cleared except for Kastor and a handful of mariners trimming the sails.

"Why you're rooted to the deck as if born asea, sir. You're a natural ye are, once you got by the puking."

I flushed with pride at my newfound mariner's legs, but the next roll of the deck sent me skittering sideways.

Orestes gave a short laugh. "Nevertheless, sir, ye best get below."

Aye, below.

PASSPORT CONTROL
Jean L. Kreiling

Charles de Gaulle Airport

"Control"? No, it was anarchy
as four lines funneled into three,
then two, all ending up inside
a maze of rope lines that defied
our hopes for just a modicum
of dignity, and then as someone poked me in the back, we heard,
from yards away, the latest word:
a uniformed official yelled,
so loudly that she'd have excelled
at drawing distant livestock near,
"All *U.S.* passports over *here*!"
Yes, in that crowded and chaotic
room—some of us near psychotic
with exhaustion and frustration—
we found new cause for irritation:
although we'd heeded every sign,
we'd waited on the wrong damned line.

THE PRIORITY LINE
David Macpherson

A while back, I found myself at the airport in the priority line at my gate. Let me confess from the beginning, I did not hold a first class ticket, nor was I a platinum, gold, ruby, diamond, or chartreuse cardholder. I'm not an active member of the military, the only group, in my opinion, which deserves priority treatment. (I've not seen many soldiers use this line—I'm guessing many military men and woman don't feel they deserve special treatment—that's their nature.) My credit card color defines me as an, at most, moderately active, middle-class traveler. I was in the wrong line by honest mistake.

I'm pretty sure most readers who have traveled by air recently can picture the side-by-side lines at the gate labeled "Priority" or "General" or some other equivalent words. I'd just stepped into the wrong line probably having been pushed by the herd of passengers, like me, rushing forward when boarding begins to be sure they can find a space for their bag in the overheads. Beyond missing the flight altogether (I prefer to arrive at the airport a few days before my flight), you don't want to be "that guy" who can't fit his bag in the overhead and has to schlep it to the front of the plane to be "gate checked." It looks incredibly awkward, the glances from those with safely stowed luggage running from pity to derision.

I found myself boxed in by priority passengers in front and behind me. My briefcase was an old backpack, my roller bag dated by its handle, and my shoes scuffed penny loafers. I was conspicuously out of place among the silk scarves and designer shoes—I clearly didn't belong. A "limbo" move to the other line I was sure would result in a call for medical assistance. My only other option was to push my frayed roller bag through the well dressed to exit the line. I decided to fake it.

As I waited, I silently practiced witty phrases that might assuage the hostile counseling I was likely to receive from the gate agent when I presented my inferior boarding pass followed by an angry message on the overhead speaker reminding passengers to board only with their assigned group, similar to the call for a price check at the pharmacy counter, "Need a price on rainbow ribbed condoms." I couldn't think of anything even vaguely humorous. During times of stress, I often revert to magical thinking—maybe the gate agent wouldn't notice. My armpits were moist as I waited for my near certain public flogging.

I've spent a lot of time ruminating about the priority line at airport gates. Most airlines (other than Southwest) use such a system. I've wondered about the line's purpose. Perhaps the traveler's experience in the priority line is better—scented air, soft music only the traveler can hear, thicker carpet. As I stood for the first time in the better line, the experience seemed exactly like the general line, most people looking inpatient or scrolling in their phone with one guy talking aloud presumably on a business call (but perhaps having an auditory hallucination about moving products quickly to San Diego—you just can't tell sometimes).

So, if the priority line experience is no different than general boarding, what's the purpose? Might different lines separate the herds creating more space for the priority folks? To do that, the lines should be far apart, and I've never seen them configured other than immediately adjacent. Despite separate lines, the herds are still mixing at the gate as best as I can tell.

Perhaps the airlines believe that priority passengers enjoy strutting their status. It's not clear why. From the behaviors I've seen, most air travelers avoid person-to-person interaction. While standing in line, you're not likely to make that key contact that sets your career soaring. And if the reason for the priority line is to allow the well to do to advertise their wealth, is the audience receptive? I may be in the minority here, but I don't think so. I've never overheard a general passenger comment to his partner, "Doesn't the priority line make her look great!" I don't look upon the people in this line with envy or approval—they just seem to be waiting in a line that offers an identical queuing experience. In some sense, our waiting experience in the line at the gate unifies us.

Unfortunately for you, the reader, I'm not quite done. The final reason for the separate line might be to simply advertise to those without priority credentials that they too might achieve this superior status. The fact that priority passengers board first is not enough. They must believe no one is paying attention to who boards first—a separate line is a necessary visual cue. This, of course, is ridiculous—every passenger waiting to board is singularly focused on staying as far to the front of their assigned line as they can, short of physical assault, to gain position. Not paying attention might lead to the dreaded gate check or even missing the flight altogether.

My line began boarding signaled by the periodic "ding, ding" of the scanner. My judgment—public humiliation versus successful deception—was at hand. When my time came, the gate agent looked at me in line and held up her hand like a traffic cop. She knows! She walked toward me. I had the urge to run. My heart was pounding.

She reached up, and, in one simple motion, switched the signs on the two lines—I was back home in "General."
I handed her my slightly moist boarding pass. "Ding, ding."

A CONVERSATION WITH MATTHEW P. MAYO

Lowestoft Chronicle

Matthew P. Mayo
(Photography: Jennifer Smith-Mayo)

Prolific author Matthew P. Mayo, who often focuses on the American West and New England, has written more than two dozen books and dozens of short stories in the past ten years. His 'grittiest moments' non-fiction books include the perennial bestseller *Cowboys, Mountain Men, and Grizzly Bears*, and his many Westerns include the 2013 Spur Award-winning novel *Tucker's Reckoning*. A frequent contributor to anthologies of fiction, Mayo's stories and essays are especially worth seeking out. His recent work can be found in *The Trading Post & Other Frontier Stories* (Five Star) and *Invigorating Passages* (Lowestoft Chronicle), both published in 2018.

Arguably, Mayo is at the height of his career and writing his best work to date. Earlier this year, he won the Spur Award, the Peacemaker Award, and the Wrangler Award for his historical novel *Stranded*, and his Roamer Western, *Timberline*, and *Blood and Ashes*, book two in The Outfit series, received glowing reviews in *Booklist*, the *Lancashire Post* and other periodicals.

In this exclusive interview with *Lowestoft Chronicle*, Mayo talks about some of his popular characters, his newest Western adventure series, his recent multi-award-winning young adult historical novel, and his exciting future projects.

Lowestoft Chronicle (LC): Matt, the last time I interviewed you, your excellent western *The Hunted* had just been published, and you were putting the finishing touches to *Double Cross Ranch*. I thought Big Charlie Chilton was an inspired choice of hero and rejoiced when he appeared again, a couple of years later, in *Shotgun Charlie*. What made you write a prequel rather than a sequel? Might he surface again someday?

Matthew P. Mayo (MPM): First of all, thanks for inviting me for an interview—it's always fun chatting with you. As for Big Charlie Chilton appearing in a prequel rather than a sequel, I recall while writing the novel that served as his first outing, *The Hunted*, that I wanted to know where he came from, so I set out to find out. As to Charlie surfacing again one day, I suspect not, at least not in that guise. That said, he's not unlike another of my protagonists I've been writing about for some time, Roamer, now appearing in a stack of short stories as well as in three novels (*Wrong Town*, *North of Forsaken*, and *Timberline*).

LC: *Shotgun Charlie* was the final novel you published with Signet. You placed the next three with Five Star, an imprint of Gale, part of Cengage Learning. Was this a deliberate switch from Signet?

MPM: I actually placed my next six novels with Five Star (the two most recent Roamer novels, as well as *Stranded: A Story of Frontier Survival*, and the three Outfit novels). It wasn't so much a calculated switch from Signet as it was their decision, as with so many publishing houses, to ratchet back their Western offerings. Fortunately, Five Star has been steadily increasing its historical-novel offerings under its "Frontier Fiction" line, which includes among others, traditional Western novels. Five Star is, it must be said, an amazing publisher to work with. The people, from editorial through art, marketing, and accounting, are all top-notch and genuinely concerned with putting out the best books they are capable of. And it shows—I'm proud to have my name on my novels through Five Star.

LC: Your western adventure series 'The Outfit' differs from your previous westerns in that instead of writing about a drifter, you have a band of heroes working together. You once described it as something like the *A-Team* of the Old West. Was this series inspired by the *A-Team* TV show or was that a marketing hook?

MPM: I'd long wanted to write something punchier, with an ensemble cast of characters. To that end, I succeeded, though as with my other books, I worked at making the characters human and not caricatures of kind and evil, and the situations tinged with possibility and not (too) outlandish. I also worked to keep excitement and raw danger never far from front-and-center. As far as the *A-Team* reference I made, it seemed like a bite-size way of describing what I had in mind for the characters and their predicaments. I had a lot of fun working on The Outfit novels, and I hope to revisit the characters—any one of them would be fun to spend more time with—at some point in the future.

LC: When you first mentioned The Outfit, a couple of years back, you were finishing up book #2 and preparing to start on book #3. At the time, the series opener, *To Hell and Back*, had yet to be published. Did you approach Five Star with the idea of a long-standing series, a 3-book series, or did you pitch them one book at a time?

MPM: I initially pitched the idea as a series to a different publisher, which they liked, but the money and terms were not favorable, so I declined and sat on the idea for a few years. Five Star liked the idea. They buy on full manuscript, not on proposal, so though it's a series, they bought the books one at a time. Each came out in successive Octobers: *To Hell and Back* (Book 1), in 2016; *Blood & Ashes* (Book 2), in 2017; and *Outlawed!* (Book 3), in 2018.

LC: The close, joshing relationship between the characters Rafe Barr and the older Cookie McGee is reminiscent of the friendship between Ty Farraday and Uncle Hob from *Double Cross Ranch*. Were Ty and Hob blueprints for Rafe and Cookie?

MPM: I think it's more of a case of me liking such relationships— the wise, older character mixing it up and offering advice to a younger, rough-but-kind mentee, of sorts. Something similar goes on between Maple Jack and Roamer—always with a bit of spice, for fun!

LC: There's an interesting development in *Blood & Ashes* when the character Susan Pendleton realizes her lifelong dream of working for the Pinkerton Detective Agency. Did Kate Warne, the first female operative to work for that agency, inspire you to make Sue a Pinkerton agent? Also, *Blood & Ashes* has echoes of The Baltimore Plot, a secessional plot to kill Lincoln, of which the mysterious Warne played a hand. Is the plot to *Blood & Ashes* loosely based on that real-life incident?

MPM: Certainly historic characters, episodes, and events help inform what I write, but I tend to use them more as ideas on which to build my own stories. Sue is becoming a strong character, more self-reliant as time rolls on, which was always my intention, but I didn't consciously use Kate Warne as a model for Sue. I thought that as an operative she could get into all manner of hijinks and raise a ruckus that men in that position might not be able to.

LC: There's a sense of resolution by the close of *Outlawed!*, and yet the series promises to continue. Do you have narrative threads in mind you're keen to pursue, or is it more a gut feeling you'll want to return to the series again at a later date?

MPM: I have a number of specific ideas for The Outfit I'd like to work with, and a pile of troubles I'd like to throw at the characters, either on their own or as part of a continuation of the ensemble. As to when I'll add more novels to The Outfit series, it's not likely to be in the near future. I'm working on a number of ideas, many of them non-Western, that I'm enjoying. But I do intend to write short stories now and again using characters from The Outfit. In fact, I'm working on one now....

LC: Like many, I'm a keen fan of your distinctive, luckless vagabond Roamer, first seen in *Wrong Town*, published by the UK publisher Robert Hale in 2008. That original Roamer adventure, revised and republished over the years (and at some point retitled *Blood Trail to Tall Pine*), still stands as one of your best tales. The follow-up, *North of Forsaken*, came out in 2017, and a third book, *Timberline*, was published last year. Why the long wait for book #2?

MPM: Thank you. I'm pleased to hear Roamer is well regarded as I enjoy spending time with him. Regarding *Wrong Town* republished as *Blood Trail to Tall Pine*—that version is a Stateside large-print version. The short answer regarding the wait for Roamer's second novel-length outing is that I was busy writing other books—non-fiction projects, short stories, novels, and more. But that doesn't mean I didn't want to jump into a new Roamer romp at every turn!

LC: Roamer and his buddy Maple Jack feature in a number of short stories, including the exceptional ghostly Christmas tale "O Unholy Night." Do you plan to write more short fiction, Roamer tales or otherwise?

MPM: No matter how much time passes between Roamer and Maple Jack adventures, as soon as I begin a new one, be it a short story or a novel, it's as if no time has passed. I love interacting with them and writing about them. And I look forward to catching up with them again soon. As for Roamer and Maple Jack shorts, yes indeed, I have, in varying stages of construction, a number of short stories, novellas, and novels featuring the duo.

I do write lots of short fiction. Much of it is waiting to find a home, some of it eventually gets teased out into something novel length. I've published several dozen short stories over the years, steampunk, crime, mystery, thrillers, horror, humor, pulpy noir, Western, barbarian, Sherlock Holmes, and more. In fact, I had a couple of short stories come out last summer. One in a Five Star anthology called *The Trading Post & Other Frontier Stories* and another in the latest anthology from Western Fictioneers called *The Untamed West*. I also have a fun bit of fiction coming out in a book in 2019, a collection of real forewords to books that don't exist. The book is to be called *Moving Forewords*, and I'm told it will contain contributions by a number of well-known celebrities (and me … go figure!).

LC: You've written numerous successful 'Grittiest Moments' nonfiction books, including the ever-popular *Cowboys, Mountain Men, and Grizzly Bears*. The novel *Stranded*—one of the most remarkable books I've read—emanates from the book chapter you wrote about Janette Riker's harrowing story of survival. It's my understanding you had very little information about Janette to go on, in which case, how difficult was it turning this brief historical account into a full-blown novel? At what point did you know you'd begun penning something extra special?

MPM: Thank you for your compliment regarding *Stranded*. The novel did come about from research I undertook for the aforementioned non-fiction book. There wasn't much information available about Miss Riker, but the information that was there was just enough, the perfect skeleton for a novel. I asked myself "what if?" and the story unfolded from there. It's funny you mention that it seems 'extra special,' because that's how I felt while I was writing it, more and more so as the story unrolled. I feel fortunate to have been the one to help tell Miss Riker's incredible story of survival. I'm also grateful and overwhelmed by the awards its earned and grand reception it's received from critics and readers.

LC: As a seasoned writer with many published books to your name, do you have a back catalog of unpublished work or do they all find a publisher?

MPM: I think most people who have been whapping the keyboard for a while have a few "trunk novels"—that is to say efforts that reside in a trunk or drawer. They can remain unseen/unsold for many reasons including market whims, lack of effort on the author's part to sell it, or…maybe they're not all that good. I have four or five novels and some short stories that are pretty much complete but haven't sold. I revisit them from time to time and vow to get them out and circulating among publishers as time permits. But they have to be good enough. Time tells all.

LC: Are you able to talk a little more on upcoming projects? Rumor has it you're working on a novel featuring William F. "Buffalo Bill" Cody. I also remember you telling me once about a YA steampunk series you were developing which stemmed from your short story 'Scourge of the Spoils.' I enjoyed that story very much when I first read it. What's the latest on the series?

MPM: The Buffalo Bill Cody novel is more of a book about other folks in which he plays an important role. It's roughed out but not completed yet—I can't wait to finish it! I have another historical YA-crossover novel all but done. It's about the Sheep Wars in Wyoming. And yes, I have the first in a planned action-heavy series based on my award-nominated steampunky/fantasy/sci-fi short story, "Scourge of the Spoils" from the DAW Books anthology, STEAMPUNK'D! I believe the coming year will bring exciting news about this novel. Stay tuned….

LC: Some years ago, you talked about slowing down in terms of writing, but in recent years you've been more productive than ever. Have your recent Spur and Wrangler Awards given you extra motivation to write?

MPM: I always wish I could spend more time on fewer projects, but the truth is I love what I do, I'm lucky to be able to do so, and with an indulgent wife, I'm able to pursue it. I write at least 2,000 words a day, and the words and pages and chapters tend to stack up when you pursue something steadily like that. The awards—eight or so for *Stranded* alone—are flattering and I'm grateful for the recognition by my fellow writers and by readers, librarians, and judges.

The real motivation to write each day comes from something that's not easy to identify. It's an urge to share ideas with people. I have more ideas for stories than I have time in life to write them, and I'm glad of it. Of course, the real trick is making certain I'm sharing stories that people want to read.

Thank you, Nicholas, for the interview. I appreciate your interest in my work.

BORDER CROSSING
Diane G. Martin

One wonders whether this side of the wall,
or that while straddling jagged stones above.
To jump or not to jump, the barren call,

or the lush in the hush of quiet, tall
misgiving? That side beckons open, rough,
though unconfined, a straight shot to the thrall,

which may prove very long or gently small.
Aside and moist, green camouflage, a grove
of cover, fecund refuge. Either sprawl

requires stout shoes and wiry nerves. The fall,
the plunge to lower depths. Release a dove
Into the wild so it can flap, not crawl.

Inside or out? Inside out. Like a brawl
of yarns, no knowing how tangled they prove
until unpicked, conundrums garble, stall

in freefall, caught within the fetus caul
that plugs the birth canal. Rough push enough,
and over the high barrier. The ball
of scraps of yarn spools round a straw-stuffed doll.

MILES OF ASPHALT
Katie Frankel

My band of women and I would always road trip back and forth across the western United States as I grew up. At first, it was to drive to California to stay for the summer, and then when we moved there, it was to drive back to Texas to visit periodically. From the time I was eight years old, I spent several days of every summer watching the burnt, yellowed grass of North Texas turn into desert. The scenery stayed brown all the way up until San Diego, with thick tumbleweeds blowing across the road just like in the Old West movies. I could see jack rabbits propelling forward on skinny legs, their long ears sticking straight up; I could always recognize this prominent feature, even all the way from the backseat of our dusty black Suburban.

At the time, I usually didn't like those seemingly never-ending car rides. The cup holders and floors would fill up with the greasy wrappers from McDonald's breakfast sandwiches, and no matter how frequently my mom would order us to throw out our trash, someone would always find a collection of rock-hard French fries under the seat weeks later. Even after the fast food trash had been cleaned out of the car to the best of our knowledge, the smell still lingered for days, making me feel nauseous every time I climbed inside.

Especially when I was younger, my grandma seemed to know that those road trips could be hard on us kids. The rise in elevation across the mountains of the desert always made my ears pop and throb in pain. Once, at a McDonald's, despite my horrid mood, she placed her bony fingers to either side of my face and kissed me, smearing my cheek with the red lipstick she always donned, even on these road trips. She then tried to cheer me up with an Oreo McFlurry.

On the second day of one of our road trips, I slunk to the tile floor inside the bathroom of a Denny's restaurant that we had stopped in, feeling sick. I was about ten, and still very susceptible to car sickness.

"Mommy said to get off the floor. It's dirty," my older sister told me after tattling on me to our mother. Slowly, I dragged myself up to my feet, wondering why I hadn't been able to just puke in the toilet already.

Returning to the table, I sat down a stared at my plateful of pancakes before vomiting long and hard into them.

"Eww," both of my sisters choked out in disgust.

My older sister was assigned the role of telling the waitress what had happened as the rest of us fled the scene.

Pulling away from the diner, I felt worse, not better, as I usually did after finally puking. "I need to stop," I begged my mom in a gasp, the motion of the car only making my nausea intensify. My twin sister complained as well, but my mom and grandma adamantly refused; we had to make our time.

A few minutes later, my twin sister and I vomited into plastic grocery bags in unison, right from the backseat.

Staying in the seedy motels along the way was a mixture of horribleness and great fun.

"What are those white stains?" I asked in naïve curiosity, pointing to a dried splattering on the floor.

My mom refused to ever let us walk around the motel rooms barefoot.

Another time, late at night in maybe west Texas or Arizona, my sisters, mom and I toted our bags in the outdoor hallway to the room we had been assigned. A group of men lingering outside stared at us as we walked, smiling and lowering their voices as we passed.

"Mommy, what time's Daddy gonna get here?" I asked

loudly, just as we'd rehearsed.

Across miles and miles over the desert, Lucinda Williams, the Cranberries, Alanis Morissette and the Dixie Chicks provided the soundtrack to our road trips. Each time a song I particularly liked was over, I knew that I would get to hear it again in another hour or so, and then an hour after that. The wind that blew in at eighty miles an hour whistled loudly every time my mom cracked her window to smoke a cigarette, temporarily interrupting the song.

When we got out of the car for gas and snacks, the heat was always so intense that I would feel my entire body pulsating. I imagined if I placed my palm on the asphalt, the skin would sizzle and boil, like the time I accidentally burned my ear with the hair straightener. On these road trips we always had at least one dog with us – usually, Buddy, an Irish Setter – and he would struggle to find an excusable burnt patch of grass to pee on.

Gas stations became scarce out in the middle of nowhere, and sometimes we had to drive far into the night before we even found a motel to stop at. My mom always had the Suburban stocked with plenty of water, "just in case." Once, probably around one in the morning, we were all just dying to pee and hadn't seen a place to stop for hours. Somewhere in West Texas, we pulled up to an isolated, abandoned concrete building, a dim light shining down on it.

"It looks like haunted out here," my sister said.

"They filmed one of the horror movies somewhere around here," my mom confirmed. She didn't say this to scare us; we all thought it was cool, and giggled loudly as we pulled down our pants, squatting down against the wall of the building as we all peed on the asphalt. There wasn't a single soul around for miles, and we probably could have done anything we wanted in that creepy Texas ghost town.

Having traveled thousands of miles, my sisters and I had

the routine down pat on who would stake claim to "the way back," or the third row seating in the car. My twin sister got it in the morning, I got it in the afternoon, and my older sister got it in the evening and into the night. This was our treasured time to lie out across the seat and sleep, without having to sit in the second row with our large dog splayed out in between two of us.

The times my grandma would come with us, she would always speed down the dusty roads like a madwoman, intent on getting us where we needed to go with no time to lose. From the driver's side back seat, I watched her red-dyed puffy hair sticking up over the headrest. Once, the flashing lights of a sheriff – a real old West sheriff, with a cowboy hat and everything – pulled us over.

"Who's going to pretend they're sick?" my mom asked urgently.

I shot my hand into the air. "Me! I can do it," I promised.

When the sheriff asked, my grandma would be racing to the closest gas station to get me some Pepto Bismol because I was about ready to spew everywhere.

After hearing the carefully recited story, the sheriff peered into the backseat. He looked so serious, his big shades covering his eyes, the mustache on his upper lip resembling a furry caterpillar. I smiled, delicately placing a hand over my mouth as I bit my cheeks hard to keep from laughing.

I got yelled at as we drove away, but I knew I wasn't in too much trouble because we still hadn't gotten a ticket. "I'm sorry," I murmured sheepishly. "I laugh when I get nervous."

As I morphed from child to preteen to teenager, we still took those road trips. I would stare out the window as we drove across the desert, a thousand stars visible in the night sky even from looking out the car window. Obsessed with horses from the time I was ten years old, I imagined climbing bareback up onto a horse and galloping across the land, nothing in my way to stop me out there in the wild West.

I could never sleep in the car as much as my sisters and even my mom could. Sometimes, late at night if it was my grandma's turn to drive, she would quietly ask, "Am I the only one awake?"

"I'm awake," I would assure her quickly, feeling special in that moment. She knew that she could count on me to keep her company up until the earliest hours of the morning.

I hated those road trips. I loved those road trips.

My last road trip happened sometime in ninth grade. I didn't know it would be the last one, of course; there's a last time for everything, but no one ever realizes when they're belting 'Drunken Angel' with their mom across the desert, or walking their Irish Setter, or kissing their speed demon grandma for the last time.

LIFE IS GRAND
Mark Halpern

Business trips call for Western rooms. They are, simply put, business-like; the furniture organizes their geometry into functionality. But this hotel's rooms, undersized and narrow "singles" every one, would be constraining to the point of oppression. At least a washitsu promised some open space, as well as the comforting scent of tatami.

"*Futon-wo shiite kudasai.*" Please lay out the futon. "*Hai wakarimashita,*" acknowledged the desk clerk. I was glad—proud—I could handle even so simple a task, after the mess I'd made so far.

On the "limited express" I'd misconstrued announcements and, drifting in and out of sleep, failed to count the stops. Not until 21:28 did I reach Hazureyama Station, but the adjacent hotel, bright and modern, stood there inviting, just as on my visit a year earlier, when I traveled from London. The New Grand, however, claimed no record of my reservation. I had, I now realized, mistakenly had my assistant book the (old) Grand.

The sympathetic clerk, experienced with such a predicament, apologized with apparent sincerity for being full up and produced a map and a thick marker, which he used to draw two big red circles. One surrounded the Grand Hotel, and the other a restaurant, the only one in walking distance still open. Twenty minutes later, having deposited my suitcase at my true hotel's front counter, I was headed toward the second big red circle, where awaited a meal I'd thoroughly forsworn. That is to say, additional to my generalized vow to forever leave behind destructive habits and relationships upon moving to Japan, I'd specifically forsworn this particular meal.

But, as I was to learn, Japan is less about leaving behind the old than embracing the new. And doing so where an odd reality keeps filtering through seductively familiar surfaces. Hence, while McDonald's here was, nutritionally, no less retarded, it turned out brilliantly advanced in smoke-free dining by local standards circa 1993. Accordingly, I left my book on one of the four tiny tables comprising the non-smoking section and went to order.

Welcome. *Eat to win?*

I beg your pardon?

Eat to win?

I beg your pardon?

Eat to win?

Excuse me, but what language are you speaking?

English. *Eat to win?*

Ah… Yes, I will eat in!

Thank you, sir. May I humbly take your order, sir?

I'd like a Big Mac Set with a large coke and large fries.

(I pay. My order is presented within twenty seconds.)

I am very sorry to have kept you waiting so long, sir.

As I start eating, an elderly man puts down his tray—bearing only a cup of coffee—on the table next to mine. He then ambles over to the restaurant's far side and plucks a large silver-colored ashtray from a stack. Once back, he places it over the no-smoking notice affixed to the surface of his table and lights up a cigarette. He sips his coffee very, very slowly. The staff watch and say nothing. He smokes one cigarette after another, and I'm guessing he does this every evening. I also say nothing.

Still, the Big Mac Set was as a Big Mac Set should be. It was perfect.

All I needed now, after the trials of the day and of three months in Tokyo, was a McDonald's apple pie. All I needed to put the world back into order was the reassuring pleasantness of eating an oblong deep-fried Hot Apple Pie out of its similarly-shaped container, with its nice smooth-surfaced cardboard, hot goop dribbling out as the pie's crispy surface crumbles.

I'd like a Hot Apple Pie.

I'm extremely sorry, sir. We are sold out of Apple Pie. Won't you take a Bacon and Potato Pie instead?

No thank you.

(Perplexity ensues at my non-acceptance that the two varietals are functionally equivalent.)

Uh… I see. Uh… Uh… I am extremely sorry, sir.

I considered ordering a Smile, a *sumairu*, at the posted price of ¥0—just to show there were no hard feelings. But that might be treated as a literal request. Humor and irony were distant goals. I was still working on not-taking-for-grantedness.

Returning to the Grand, I picked up my suitcase and rode the elevator to the top floor. There, I found a traditional *washitsu*, separated by sliding shoji from a smaller linoleum-tiled Western-style space that held a dresser, proper writing desk, and large color television. Fourteen *tatami* on the Japanese side, easily enough space for six futons placed decently apart. But the *tatami* was bare. Instead, an army cot had been wheeled onto the linoleum and unfolded beneath the fluorescent light fixture.

Excuse me, but in my room, there is a bed, rather than a futon.

Yes, that is so. Would you like another pillow or another blanket?

But when I checked in I asked you to put out a futon.

Yes, but you are a foreigner.

I am a foreigner, but I would like to sleep on a futon. That is why I asked for the Japanese room.

The manager instructed me to set up a bed.

But I asked for a futon.

The manager said you probably wanted a bed. Would you like another pillow or another blanket?

When I checked in, I specifically said, in Japanese, "please lay down a futon."

Yes. I told the manager, but he instructed me to set up the bed.

May I please speak with the manager?

I'm sorry. He is away now and will return at eleven o'clock.

Could you please take away the bed and lay out a futon for me?

I will have to ask the manager. Would you like another pillow or another blanket?

No thank you. I do not need another pillow or blanket.

I understand. Please let me know if there is anything else I can help you with.

Please ask the manager to let you take away the bed and put out a futon for me.

Yes. I see. I'm sorry, but I will have to wait until the manager gets back. He will return at eleven o'clock.

Is a customer who takes a Japanese-style room allowed to sleep on a futon?

Yes. That is so.

I am a customer in a Japanese-style room. Please let me sleep on a futon.

But you are a foreigner and the manager said that for foreigners, beds are better.

If there is a foreigner customer who takes a Japanese room and that foreigner customer asks to sleep on a futon, is he allowed to sleep on a futon?

Yes. That is so.

I am a foreigner customer who took a Japanese room and am asking to sleep on a futon. Will you please lay out a futon?

Ah… Yes. Yes, I see. Yes. I will lay out a futon. Yes.

Okay, please do so.

Of course, sir. I will lay out the futon as soon as the manager returns. Until he returns, I have to stay at the front desk, since no other employees are on duty. He will return at eleven o'clock.

Okay. I will come back later.

Goodbye, sir.

I fell back in retreat. The McDonalds—a table midway between the chain-smoking elderly man, still sipping coffee, and some boisterous teenagers, only half of whom were smoking. I ordered a Bacon and Potato Pie from the same counter clerk. I was certainly embarrassed, and he may have been too, for all I know. His words were as polite as before, but his face was flat and emotionless.

The Bacon and Potato Pie had the same shape and nice packaging as the Apple Pie. It was perfect. I ordered another.

The teenagers left gradually and the smoke thinned. Eventually, it was just me and the elderly man. Finally, he too got up and left, pouring a little cold coffee into his ashtray, extinguishing the smoldering butt at the top of the mound. My watch said 22:59. Closing time.

Back at the front desk, the manager stood at stiff attention.

I humbly welcome you back, sir.

Thank you. Is my room ready now?

May I humbly ask that you condescend to wait just a few minutes longer while we humbly finish the preparations? Won't you graciously sit down and relax?

Okay. Thanks.

(I sit and read my book. The clerk appears and confers with the manager.)

Sir, I take the liberty of humbly advising you that your room is now ready.

Thank you.

May I take the further liberty, sir, of wishing you a good night?

The folding cot had vanished. Laid out on the *tatami* was a futon covered by a fluffy duvet, both with a pattern of pretty flowers in blue and green. The duvet had been turned down. And just visible between the futon and *tatami* was a thick, soft-looking under-mat. Nearby, sat a stained wooden tray on which rested a lacquered thermos-type pitcher of cold water and an empty glass.

I got ready for bed and quickly fell into a deep slumber. Because I'd drunk the whole pitcher of water—owing to my earlier consumption of two deliciously salty Bacon and Potato Pies, not to mention the salty Big Mac and salty large fries—it was inevitable I'd need to visit the washroom in the middle of the night. But when I did so, I was not fully awake and a dream lingered on.

(The McDonald's counter clerk, beaming, hands me a glistening, gargantuan bacon triple cheeseburger, without any wrapping. It vanishes from a silver platter. I am aware that I have eaten it.)

I humbly inform you, sir, that you have been awarded the Grand Prize.

That's because I eat to win. Draw a big red circle around me. On the map of Japan.

(My pale blue futon is my magic carpet, hovering gently over a deep green forest. I sit bolt upright, dressed like Aladdin. An express train flies by. I lick my fingers, all greasy from my bacon triple cheeseburger, and then pick up my coke bottle. Cigarette smoke billows out and a giant hotel manager magnificently emerges, wearing a turban.)

I am deeply sorry to have kept you waiting so long, Master. May I be so bold as to take the further liberty of humbly requesting that you condescend…?

In the morning, I awoke, fully, to the fresh, astringent fragrance of *tatami* and to a triangle of warm sun streaming onto my body through the sliver between the curtains in the

Western part of the room. I felt completely refreshed and that my night must have been filled with the most pleasant dreams of all kinds. As to the previous day's struggles, my recollections were dominated by a self-satisfaction at having been able to resolve the futon issue so successfully.

After my usual morning routine and preparations for meeting with a local customer, I went to breakfast at the first-floor restaurant. From behind the front desk, a cheerful young woman called out good morning. The night staff was no longer on duty.

The restaurant was spacious and airy for a "business hotel"—meaning any hotel a salaryman might use for business travel on a limited budget but preferably not for a pleasant family vacation. I ordered the Western breakfast, suppressing all thoughts concerning healthy lifestyles. Soon, came strong coffee, followed by bacon and two scrambled eggs and, on the same plate, a good quantity of fried potatoes and a mix of broccoli and carrots that were not especially overcooked. On the side were a green salad and white bread toast with lots of real butter. A small bowl held colorful, rectangular peal-back packets of jam. I retrieved four, each a different type, and spread their contents on my toast.

I polished off everything, including a refill of fresh coffee. Then, after packing my suitcase and calling my office, I made my way to the front desk.

Good morning, sir. Will you be checking out?

Yes, please.

Certainly, sir. Just a moment, please… *(Twelve seconds elapse.)* I am very sorry to have kept you waiting. Here is your bill. I hope everything was to your satisfaction.

Is this amount correct? *(It was the equivalent of 64 US dollars.)* I stayed in the large-size *washitsu*, had the breakfast and made a long-distance call.

Yes, sir. I am sorry, but I do think the bill is correct. Is there any problem?

Not at all. I just wanted to check.

Thank you very much. Here is your change, sir. Please come again.

My meeting went splendidly. I returned to Tokyo bearing a big new order, triumphant, arranging to visit Hazureyama again two weeks later with Bjorn, one of our tech guys. He would deal with their tech guys; I would just make the introduction.

When the day came, Bjorn and I arrived early afternoon, but it seemed his meeting would spill over into the following morning. Before going onward, I recommended he take a *washitsu* at the Grand Hotel, especially as he gets a flat *per diem* for expenses. My courtesy calls at other regional clients went well and, after some sightseeing over the weekend, I headed home.

On Monday, I asked Bjorn how he'd liked the Grand, but he'd stayed instead at the New Grand. The (old) Grand refused his reservation, saying they weren't equipped for foreigners. Bjorn pressed them, even mentioning his colleague's wonderful experience there.

The woman on the phone was profusely apologetic. She said the no-foreigner policy had been implemented only recently and was truly unfortunate. She paused before continuing. Just two weeks earlier, she said, there had been an "incident."

CENTERPIECES AT THE INN
James B. Nicola

In the lobby, twelve bell jars of potpourri,
one on each table, greet the guested world,
their burrs, cones, stems and leaves, uniformly
blue, as they've been dyed, the dried leaves, curled.

One guest grunts a comment about the bell jar
at the last vacant table, takes his place
for breakfast, and is joined. A foreigner,
he is not understood. And yet his face

shines like the rest's, reflecting leaves and burrs.
Two ladies have applied blue eye shadow
and scented themselves like the conifers,
whose heirs they'll feed one day, like all the guests,
in random forests or a cultured row,
between their travels and their good nights' rests.

NOISE

Brian James Lewis

This morning I woke up to two birds mimicking car alarms. They had it down perfect. One bird was doing the more European "Beew beew beew!" and continued into the exciter mode that most of those alarms feature. The other bird did the more meat and potatoes repetitive horn honk thing. "Honk! Honk! Honk! Honk!" Despite being annoyed, I couldn't help but be impressed by these birds for learning what they hear daily in our neighborhood.

Every weekday morning, I am required by marital etiquette to start my wife's car so that it can heat up to roughly the temperature inside an industrial toaster before she drives away in it. I know that it's wasteful to leave a car running for fifteen minutes just to warm up the interior, but that is what my wife demands. If you want to argue with her first thing in the morning, I wish you luck. For safety purposes, I'll hide in the bushes until she drives away, and then call an ambulance to scrape what's left of you off the ground.

My desires in the morning are to drink coffee and avoid any kind of argument. To do that, I stagger out to the car in my highly stylish winter morning attire of pajamas and large boots, topped off by a huge jacket. As I approach the car, I yell and hit the clicker on the key fob. I always yell when I'm going to start any of our vehicles because there is a very high concentration of feral cats in our neighborhood and the last thing I want to do is get one of them caught in the engine. Nobody with a dead cat under their hood ever has a good day.

Once inside the car, I turn the key, which results in the car starting and a blare from the radio. "Come on down to Ralph

Burns Toyota! We got over four thousand cars! That's FOUR THOUSAND CARZZZZ!" Why do car ads always shout at us? Do they think we're hard of hearing or incompetent? "JOE BLOW AUTO HAS GOT YOUR CAR IN STOCK RIGHT NOW! YES, NOW! AT SIX IN THE MORNING!!!" Maybe they do it to tear our eyes away from the plethora of electronic devices most people have going even if their trip only consists of driving three blocks total for milk and a box of doughnuts.

The laws against texting don't seem to be accomplishing much. To avoid it, the texters are just keeping their phones in their laps or on the passenger seat. I'm not sure which is worse, a person looking at the road with a phone near their face, or a person barreling down the road while staring into their lap. Neither is a good thing, but at least the person looking straight ahead might have a slight advantage.

While phones are bad, don't even get me started on the minivans that are rolling entertainment centers! The driver is trying to watch the DVD screen over his head while the GPS navigator shows and tells him where to go. His passenger is poking her phone in his face with a fun picture on Facebook and his ten-year-old daughter in the backseat is gasping at her tablet and saying, "Uh-Oh! That's not supposed to happen!" That person is beyond distracted and is driving on reflexes alone.

This is something that old people can't fall back on. If they get confused in their own homes, their chances aren't going to get any better in a moving vehicle. Throw in a cell phone and you've got a recipe for disaster. What's the deal with old people and their phones, anyway? They never let a call go to voicemail! They might be going around a traffic circle, or in line at the grocery store. It doesn't matter. They just whip that baby out and start talking as if they've entered a private phone booth. "Hullo? Hullo? Oh hiya, Ralph. How's your nuts today? Hurting? You sure you're not just sitting on them? Ol' Burt

Sullivan found out that was his problem! Pissing blood? Well, that's no good!" This can go on for a significant amount of time. As the cashier attempts to get the man's attention, the old guy gets all testy. "Hang on Ralph, some stupid kid is asking me for money!"

Apparently, old people don't trust technology to transport their voices loudly enough, so they usually bellow into their phones. While it can be entertaining at times, there are moments when it can be downright disgusting. I'll never forget the woman in the booth behind us at the Blue Dolphin Diner telling the person on the phone a very graphic account of her venereal disease problems. "There's so much pus and it smells soooo bad! I'm all itchy too!" She had me shouting for the check and telling the waitress very firmly that I most certainly did not want any banana cream pie for dessert today!

I usually just listen to music while I'm driving my car. Mine is old enough that it plays CDs and cassettes. Hey! How about that for cool? Yeah, I'm not real modern. Most of the time things go fine. I listen to music, drive, and usually get where I'm going without incident. But problems come along when I need to change a CD or cassette. Sometimes the player isn't ready to let them go and there's a bit of a wrestling match as the light turns green and people honk their horns to make me get going. I respond by throwing the offending CD out the window and turn on the radio instead. The Pop music stations where I live are pretty sad and seem to have a fixation on Justin Bieber songs. So I suffer through some sort of whiney whispering, hoping that the next song will be by Meghan Trainor, but instead, all I get for my trouble is:

"C'MON DOWN TO ROD'S ROCKIN' RIDES FOR THE SALE OF A LIFETIME! NO DOWNPAYMENT REQUIRED! FREE HOT DOGS AND BALLOONS FOR THE KIDS! THIS SATURDAY ONLY! COME ONE, COME ALL, TO ROCKIN' RODS AUTO MALL! ALL

YOU GOTTA DO IS…Click!"

Ahh! Listen to that silence. Isn't it wonderful?

THE BUZZING
Philip Barbara

Sachs had a new idea: To shoo the geese off the lawn, he bought a cardboard cutout of a fox that stood two feet tall on hind legs. The fox had reddish-orange fur, white whiskers, a bushy tail with a white tip, and slanting eyes that gave it a menacing, cunning air. He affixed the cutout to a pole, and, when the ground had softened from its winter freeze, used a rubber mallet to pound the pole into the ground. The fox shivered in the late April breeze, becoming more lifelike and thus more effective. Dozens of birds glided above the lawn that rolled down to Comity Pond. As they flew lower, they spread both wings and extended their legs to alight gently on the water. They avoided the lawn.

Sachs relaxed in a folding chair on his small dock and enjoyed the success of his new guardian. There would be no more running after the birds with an umbrella, thrusting it open and pulling it closed, or banging a big metal pot with a wooden spoon. He'd no longer have to sidestep bird droppings. With the fox, the lawn and pond were once again a peaceful, pastoral place for an aging man to sit in the sun and read the books he always wanted to read or to do nothing but drift from daydream to daydream.

Every spring for years the geese's droppings had destabilized the lawn's chemistry. Summer vacationers still used the lawn even though it had been disfigured with a thousand blemishes, spots of brown amid the green. When Sachs retired a year ago from his job as a Middle School Principal, he set about finding a humane solution. He called the Shore Conservatory for advice, left a message but got no call back. Next, a search on his computer led him to a site that sold 'faux predators.' He chose the fox. By summer the lawn would be a brilliant emerald carpet, cut each week so precisely that no blade of grass would ever rise above its peers.

It wasn't that he didn't like the birds. To the contrary, he did. Their easy grace and joyful choreography on the water charmed Sachs. The geese and other waterfowl floated freely on the pond and replenished themselves before resuming their journey up the Mid-Atlantic Coast to Canada. Their freedom was akin to the spontaneity he enjoyed in retirement. From his chair, Sachs operated a wireless remote device. When the birds gathered in a chevron formation like a proud feathery armada, he pushed a joystick on his remote and sent a model cabin cruiser toward them. The boat's motor made a buzzing sound, but at low speed, the buzzing didn't frighten the birds. It allowed him to get close, almost to join the flock. He pressed a button to activate a camera built into the bow of the boat and snapped a photograph. He followed one bird around and took close-ups of its beige and gray tail feathers. He captured the profile of another bird, the white patches on its face and its bill filling his screen. Within an hour, he recorded a dozen still photos for an album and several videos bursts.

Sachs lived in a summer cottage he bought decades ago when his family was young. The cottage was one of a dozen set in an arc that closed in the two-acre lawn that rolled to the pond's edge. When his wife was alive, the two of them tended an herb garden and their children played on the lawn. Now he lived in the cottage year-round. Young families rented the cottages during warm weather. His son and his grandchildren were planning a visit, and he visualized the kids racing across the lawn to greet playmates from the previous summer. They'd play badminton and Wiffle ball. Maybe this would be the year his grandson accomplished what Sachs' son had done so long ago – toss a Frisbee across the pond safely to a friend. If it landed in the water again, his son would fetch it in the family kayak as he had before.

The warmth of the sun passing through Sachs' khaki pants and windbreaker made him drowsy. He navigated the model boat back to the dock, shut the motor, and rested the remote in his lap. He closed his eyes and drifted into thought. Migrating is so universal, driven by natural and man-made forces; it can be easy for wildlife but not so for people. It was a blessing that he would grow old in one place. He rested his chin on his chest and fell asleep.

Sachs was startled awake by what sounded like an industrial-sized leaf blower. Yet he didn't see one – what was that buzzing? He looked around, stopping for a moment to admire the tender green of the maple and oak trees that were beginning to bud. Then he spotted his neighbor across the pond, holding a remote device much like his own and using it to control a model biplane. When he flew it higher, straight up, two hundred feet high, the sound from the engine rose to an irritatingly high-pitched buzzing. The biplane was outmoded by today's designs yet could maneuver like a modern warplane. The neighbor sent it into a nosedive toward the birds, and a dozen of them cried and scattered. Then he brought the plane level so that it skimmed above the pond's surface, heading straight toward another group. They flapped their wings and flew off.

"Why are you chasing the birds away?" Sachs called out. The neighbor had moved in last June, and other than giving him a welcoming wave across the pond, Sachs had not befriended him.

"They're in my garden. They're soiling my patio. I'm getting rid of them."

"But the water is their natural refuge. If they're not safe there, then where?"

"Too many of them."

"They'll be on their way soon enough."

"Tomorrow there'll be a new flock. It's as if the same birds are here for weeks. They're a nuisance."

Ironic that this guy should call the birds a nuisance. Every weekend last summer, loud rock music and laughter from youthful parties on his patio had reached Sachs' cottage well past midnight, forcing him to close his bedroom windows and shut out the mating calls of bullfrogs, the pleasing scent of salt air, and the rhythmic pounding of the nearby ocean – all of which contributed to his usual restful slumber.

"I wish you wouldn't chase them away."

"They're dull and dirty, not a bright color on them."

Sachs saw the regal beige and shimmering white feathers in his pictures. "If you saw the close-ups I've taken, you'd see them differently."

"They might be beautiful individually. But as a group they're ugly."

"I'll send you some photos," Sachs said. To see them up close was to appreciate them. He watched the neighbor return his attention to his handheld remote. The model plane's motor buzzed louder as he powered it straight up and then flew it in wide concentric circles as if hunting for prey. Suddenly the plane dove straight for a few birds sheltered among reeds rising from a mudflat. The birds squawked and flew away, except for one little bird that was too young to fly. Sachs saw this and worried a real red fox would get it. He went to help but as he approached, the bird flapped its wings madly and skittered deeper into the reeds.

Sachs returned to his cottage, obtained his neighbor's email address from a community association register, and sent the pictures. Then he called the Shore Conservatory for advice but was again directed to voicemail.

The next morning Sachs found the little bird's mangled carcass on the mudflat, its feathers scattered. He fumed. The guy couldn't understand migration patterns, the Conservatory didn't return a concerned citizen's phone call, and he hadn't saved the poor bird, concerned, as he had been, about getting his loafers muddy. Sachs marched around the pond, through private back yards, squeezing around carefully trimmed hedges, determined to tell his neighbor how people in seaside communities should behave. As a school principal, he'd always been able to contain his ire and had been a judicious arbiter when disputes between students or among faculty were brought to him. But now, chest puffing with indignation, he was prepared for a fight.

When his neighbor came to the door, Sachs let loose without a greeting: "Loud rock music from your house last summer violated the noise ordinance. I didn't call the police. Your buzzing plane violates it now. I'll put up with it. But your ill-treatment of this wildlife must stop."

His neighbor, arms akimbo, said: "You have your fox. I have my plane."

Sachs was momentarily stunned. The jerk had just called him a hypocrite. Sachs' fox was a benign trick, whereas his neighbor had made a nasty sport out of chasing the birds away. He was a predator, and not a faux one. There could be no reasoning with him.

Sachs turned and walked away without another word, shaking his head at the absurdity of the situation. Still feeling unsettled when he reached his cottage, he again called the Shore Conservatory for advice. He was encouraged when, finally, he reached an agent, who promised to come by.

The next morning, Sachs explained the situation to the agent. The man, who said he'd been with the Conservatory his entire career, replied, "There's no law forcing a citizen to accept the birds."

"Damn it. But there are rules about noise. I'll accept his annoying buzzing," Sachs said. "Can't he fly his plane without terrorizing the birds?"

The agent shrugged. "You'll have to settle this dispute with him." As he turned to leave, he added, "Wish you guys weren't making such a big issue of this."

Sachs couldn't expect anything from anybody. He alone had a decision to make. He could take the fox down and allow the birds to roam on his lawn. But no, he couldn't do that; they'd undo his efforts and ruin the lawn for his grandchildren. He was stuck.

In the end, Sachs decided to keep the fox and just be patient. He had seen over the years that most problems between people, with a little goodwill, could be resolved. He'd meanwhile send new photos of individual birds to his neighbor to nourish a change of heart. It was sunny and calm, and he went to the dock, sat in his chair and turned on the remote. Now the battery had run down. But he just wasn't going to let a loss of power ruin his day. He settled deeper in his chair, looked around and enjoyed the moment.

SONG OF THE HIGHWAY
Sharon Frame Gay

I heard it again last night, the whine of tires, ebbing and flowing along the tarmac under a roaming moon. Inside where memories sleep, the highway sings its lullaby.

I yearn to stop in a goodbye town before dawn paints it with regret, watch dogs wander barren streets, shattered glass glinting along the shoulder as we pull over, cigarette butts and bottles lying in a ditch. The wind feels different as it blows across a new horizon, the scent of early spring riding the dust into town.

Anonymous, we can choose to be scowling stranger or smiling patrons of the smoke-filled cafe. Sliding into a booth, the red seat cracked and worn, I read the festive menu covered in plastic, gaze at pictures of hotcakes and eggs over easy, and glasses of orange juice, bitter on the tongue.

In the corner is a jukebox, filled with songs from yesterday. A quarter buys a memory, a dollar buys you grief. It's enough to sit and listen, watch the trucks go by, gearing down, then speeding up as they lope along a spawning river of highway.

Back on the road, windows down, dust clogging our nostrils and staining the dashboard, I sit, feet up, head lolling, as telephone poles mark time in endless waves. The Panhandle of Texas, forlorn and spare, creates mirages in the distance. When we catch up, they disappear into grit and lonesome sky.

Turning east, heading back, the stretches of deserted land give way to higher hills and scrub. Then the oasis of town appears on the other side of the ridge, trees and grass fighting the Texas heat.

Another small town, this one bustling with the mundane of

every day. Morning is coated with heat, pushing the night to the other side of the world. Beat up pickups roam the street, Indian kids in the back, peering out from under a tarp that flutters and flaps. An old man steps out of a dismal shop, ducks under an ice cream sign, and shuffles down the sidewalk.

Inside a store, the air is redolent with grease and coffee, cheap plastic and car fresheners, little green trees that never once smelled like pine. I ask for the restroom key, carry the plank of wood and head outside, around back to an ominous door that is buckling on one side as though it wants to detach and flee. The sink is rusty, trickling water plays a sad ballad. I stand and pee, the toilet seat covers used up long ago, trash can overflowing.

On the wall are an old tampon box and an even older condom display. Twenty-five cents will get you knocked up or happy, weigh the dice, toss them, go back outside and take a breath.

Why is it that heartache sometimes feels like joy? What is it about the highway that makes my eyes grainy from lack of sleep, and blood thunder with hope? Maybe we've known sorrow so long it's an old friend who welcomes us back, giddy with relief to find us again. I want to kneel, kiss the tarmac, feel it's grit between my lips. Then spit on it in despair.

Instead, we pile into the car and toss gravel as the car swings west again.

MY KNEE HAD AN ITCH
Richard Charles Schaefer

The sun is the blaze. Earth's gravity is the rope tying me to the beach chair, which is the stake. There was no trial to speak of, and yet I burn. 'SPF 50' my tan ass. I toss myself in the ocean to see if I float.

It rained the whole drive down from Chattanooga but hasn't rained since my first sunrise in Miami, four days ago. Denise wondered why I drove instead of flying, and everyone else wondered why I was coming to Miami at all. My coworkers vacation in places like Charleston, Orlando, and Panama City Beach. I shared Interstate 75-South with mini-vans from Michigan, full of families peering out from between flip-flops and pool toys slipping out of tote bags, the spilled innards of relaxation.

"Are you meeting someone there?" Denise asked. "Or maybe *hoping* to meet someone there?" While she and I Skyped, I was sitting at my home office in North Chattanooga, looking out my window at a tree that looked undeniably like a spider; doubly troubling was the fact that it had far more than eight legs and I couldn't shake the feeling that it was moving towards my home. Since there were no Amazon Prime eligible axes that seemed adequate for self-defense, I booked the hotel room in South Beach instead. How could I explain it to Denise? Ishmael wanted to knock off hats; I wanted to deforest Lookout Valley.

But, anyway, the question, whether it's coming from Denise or one of my coworkers, really comes down to a critique of my audacity in traveling alone, and they don't expect an answer. So I spared Denise an explanation of the alien flora in Chattanooga; I do describe to her watching iguanas and vendors climb the palm trees, the former to disappear into the tufts at the base of the fronds, the latter to return with coconuts. I relate details of drunken couples' bickering at sidewalk restaurants across from Lummus Park and the way green parrots mimic them with airborne arabesques and flourishes as they squawk.

"Isn't it lonely?" she asked yesterday. The only people here who look lonely aren't alone; the lonely ones are the people staring into the watered-down universe at the center of the $45 mixed drinks they're sharing with friends and insignificant others who seem oblivious to the dejection.

"It's perfect," I said.

I flip in the water and turn my face toward the sky; maybe I can't float, exactly, but it takes minimal effort to avoid sinking.

The woman in the next stall is muttering platitudes to herself like someone in a movie talking to their reflection, borrowing from the 'pull yourself together' school of bracing, verbal slaps. I can see her wet shorts and bathing suit bottom rolled around her ankles, her bare feet shaking with just the tips of her toes touching the ground. I own the same bikini, though it's not the one I'm wearing today. The music that was playing in the lobby is also playing here in the bathroom off the hotel bar, a Spanish version of "It's a Man's World."

"This was a mistake," she says. "A mistake." So the pep talk didn't work.

If I've ever talked to myself in a bathroom stall, I certainly can't remember doing so; I'm tempted to try it now, but if I do, this lady will think I'm talking to her, so I keep quiet. We're four blocks north of my hotel on Ocean Drive, and, although this woman was possibly drinking here, I doubt she's staying in this hotel either.

She starts sobbing, then bangs on the sides of the stall once. I'm about to ask her if she's okay when I hear a trickle of urine hitting the tile and see it running toward my own feet, so I hurry out.

A man with a bright red nose and an orange bathing suit stops me at the bar.

"Was my friend in there?" he asks.

"Probably," I say.

"Either she was, or she wasn't," he says.

"There was someone in there. I don't know if it was your friend."

"It *was*," he says, either defensive or offended; it's hard to say.

———— ✦ ————

The placement of my hotel room's two mirrors—one wall-mounted, the other freestanding and full length—and one long window seemed arbitrary at first, but if I stand in the corner just behind the door and face the room, I can see the bed, the sky, and both mirrors, each reflecting the bed and the sky, and none of them capturing me.

I imagine three of myself lying on three beds, imagine six eyes staring at the corner I'm standing in. If I could set aside temporality, I could be the ghost in my own eaves. Instead, I sit down on the edge of my bed and look out at the roof of the neighboring hotel: men in hard hats, the tops of palm trees visible past the scaffolding across the front of the building, two doves mating on the corner of the stucco.

The sun is nowhere near setting, and the AC has been running non-stop against the April heat. As a kid in Massachusetts, we used air conditioning intermittently for the few weeks in the summer that really needed it, and almost never at night. I find it stifling how this unit never clicks off, but less stifling than the humidity that would suffocate the room like gauze shoved into a sucking wound if it did.

I slip out of my bathing suit and into a bra and dress and fall back on the bed I'll be sleeping in for the next month. I wonder how many people's bulks have contributed to this mattress's sag by force or simple gravity; for now, it's all mine, until Denise gets here in two and a half weeks. We'll share it like the beds we sometimes shared when we were children until I got frustrated with her faking violent dreams to twist more of the blankets onto herself and returned to my own bed. Until I learned that the night terrors she was thrashing through were real. I don't know how my sister can remain in Salem.

When I moved to Chattanooga, with no prospects to speak of, I think I expected her to follow me there. After a year or two, when I'd established a steady enough career to bear the weight of describing it to my family—Project Manager, sure, sounds impressive—I extended an official invitation to Denise to join me. She promised to think about it, and I never brought it up again. She's visited Chattanooga twice in the three years since, and I visit Massachusetts once a year for the Fourth of July, about a third as often as I visit Miami, though never for a full month before. And this is the first time I've asked Denise to join me.

I close my eyes and try to find the feel of the afternoon sun amidst the chill of the air conditioning, but it's as impossible as taking a sip of a Bloody Mary and spitting out just the vodka. I keep my eyes shut anyway; the hazy shade of darkness is the same as the red that hides inside the blacks of old Polaroids.

When I hear the knock, it sounds like it's coming from the window, so I assume it's a dream, and I ignore it. However, it's actually coming from the door, and I'm awake.

"I didn't think you were here," the maid says when I open the door. She's holding two Tupperware containers.

"I put on the 'do not disturb' sign."

"I thought you weren't here. I'll go. I'll go."

"Well, no, I guess since you're here, you can come in. You don't need to make my bed, but you can take the trash, I guess."

"No, no, I'm on my break. I'll go."

"Well, wait. If you're on your break," I say, "why are you coming in my room?"

"Ahh," she says, and gestures toward the window. One of the construction workers on the neighboring roof is waving at us. I look at the food she's holding.

"Oh, Novio?" I ask.

"Hahaha, no, he is my brother. I bring him his lunch."

"Oh," I say. The guy in the hard hat is still waving.

"These windows don't open, though. They're locked. Uh, bloqueado?"

"Oh right, right," the maid says, "saltadors. But I can open it. If you don't mind?"

"That's fine," I say.

She steps around my bathing suit and other clothing on the floor and uses a small key to unlock the window.

"Hola, hola," she shouts across the gap. There are maybe six feet between the buildings. She swings her arm back and forth underhand to indicate she's going to toss the Tupperware, and when she does it hits the side of the other building and bursts open before falling out of sight. A red stain splatters the stucco. It looks like marinara sauce, probably homemade. The maid quietly closes the window again without locking it as her brother laughs and looks down at the ground where the Tupperware must have landed.

"I'll bring you fresh towels," she mutters and hurries out of the room. Her brother is still standing there on the neighboring roof, pointing at me and smiling. No, pointing at the second Tupperware she left on my windowsill. I think about how I'd have to calculate for wind, how the other roof is slightly higher than this one, the awkward way I'd have to stick my arm out the window to get a good angle. I lower the blinds and set the chain on my door.

———— ✦ ————

Miami nights shine further into the world's corners than Tennessee's sun can. Maybe it's because the days here provide the soul's battery with enough charge to last until the next dawn. In Chattanooga, as it was in Massachusetts, the sunset signals a flipping of signs from 'open' to 'closed' in the glazed-over storefront windows of people's eyes; you can wander from face to face looking for someone still open to provide some much-needed provision that's hard to name until you find it, and you rarely do.

On South Beach, I can get that provision just by walking near a stranger, without ever saying a word to him or her or even making eye contact. Because, whatever that commodity is, it isn't really coming from them; the mere proximity to other hearts is enough to amplify the beat of my own.

On the other hand, it's possible that the nocturnal energy here is just because I'm surrounded by tourists celebrating their freedom to sleep in tomorrow by getting hammered. It's probably a mix of the former and the latter, though a watered down one.

I decide to wander away from the beach itself, heading, out of habit, toward the Lincoln Road Mall and its many blocks of shoe stores, fashion ranging from the bootleg to the beyond-reproach, and restaurants with minuscule storefronts and sizeable outdoor eating areas in the middle of the pedestrian-only street. Habit takes me further, to the only bookstore in the world where I'll willingly pay cover price for a book (and not just because I've seen people attempt to steal $300 plus art books from them on more than one occasion). I bypass the new arrivals and art books (I've been here twice on this trip already) and head into the children's room in the back. I'm alone in it, as I usually am.

There is a book I only half-remember from when I was a child, and I have an equally halved memory of seeing it from the corner of my eye in this room on a previous visit. Somewhere, here, is the missing piece of that fraction of a fraction, some part of my childhood that must be worth remembering simply because I don't.

I sought this book out consciously, once, in Massachusetts, a birthday gift for Denise's daughter. I described what I could remember of it (a young witch, a castle, an evil cat, many talking cats who weren't evil, and a post-modern tone) to, first, a bookseller, and then to Denise (who surely must have read it too), and finally to my mother, thinking it might have been an obscurity absconded from her childhood collection. None knew what I was describing.

The memory is more a texture than anything else, no keywords unique enough to string together into a Google search. The cats will only let the main witch pet them with her right hand (if at all), for her left, her casting hand, will shock them every time it touches them. Ultimately, she defeats the evil cat by scratching him between the ears with her left hand, effectively giving him shock therapy that renders him benign.

Denise insisted, when I described this to her, that it was from a story that *I* wrote (if that were true, which it's not, it's no surprise my mother wouldn't remember). However, I can remember the feel and smell of the pages (stiff almost to the point of breaking and dusty, respectively), the way the font looked, the width of the margins. When I close my eyes, I can almost see the copyright page, the crest of the publisher and the publication year just out of focus. Mostly, I remember the way the story transported me; I can still feel the way its world's gravity pushed me down in my bed as I read, the way its rules seemed to make more sense than those I had to live by (though, of course, I remember none of that liberating constitution now), the way the characters spoke truth even when they were afraid. Surely, nothing I wrote myself could move me that way, any more than I can make myself laugh by tickling my own feet.

I skim the shelves, but can't find anything like what I'm seeking. I grab a few postcards from the rack by the bathroom and buy them, so I don't seem too suspicious for skulking through the children's room. One of the postcards is a portrait of Frida Kahlo, and the others are multiple copies of a daguerreotype picturing a cat wearing reading glasses.

———— ✦ ————

"My knee had an itch," the caption says apologetically, and, in the photo, she does have one hand touching her bare thigh, ostensibly reaching toward the supposed itch, the other hand curled up and pointing at her cleavage. The photo is of one of my coworkers, wearing a bikini on the beach in Destin, on the Gulf Coast. She's tagged in other photos posted by the two friends she's on vacation with, but she posted this one herself. I'd caption it differently: "We all get itches."

I scroll past the photo and take a sip of my Cuban coffee. The tables around me are filled with families and couples eating dinner; the restaurant's staff is fluent in as many languages as the patrons can throw at them, though they don't wear their countries of origin on their nametags, like at least one other place along Lincoln Road.

My waiter was surprised when I spoke to him in English; I wonder where he thinks I'm from, or if he was merely trying to flatter me. Somehow, "where do you think I'm from?" is just as combative a question as "who do you think you are?" I can't imagine asking either question without shaking someone from the lapels while I do.

I return to the photo of my coworker, to a smile broad enough to reach the nosebleed seats of her dating app of choice; I'm sure her smile's aim is true, even if its targets are questionable. This coworker was among those who imposed scandalous subtexts upon my solo trip to Miami, winkingly telling me that she was planning a trip too. A "girl's trip," referring to the "girlfriends" undertaking the journey with her; I've never taken a girl's trip, never referred to friends as girlfriends. I'm not the prude this coworker half-presumed to be testing the boundaries of with her innuendo; I neither begrudge her her lust nor put a gag on my own. Unlike her, I'm also not afraid to be alone.

I take another sip of my coffee and lock my phone, return it to my bag. I'm thinking again about that book. I remember seeing a neighborhood cat stunned by a light blow from a passing car when I was young. I lifted the cat from the gutter and brought it to my mother. For some reason, I told her it had been struck by lightning. She took it to the vet; it recovered from both its real and imaginary injuries, and we adopted it.

There are a notebook and pen in my purse; I start to write down the memory, my momentum repeatedly disrupted by recalling more detail as I go, trying to capture it all. Trying to remember the name of the vet, I tap the pen on the edge of the page, and it slips from my fingers, landing in the small aisle between the next table and mine.

As I lean down to grab the pen, a waitress rushes by with four bottles of beer in her hands, and I bump her thigh. The beers foam a little, but nothing spills.

"Sorry, my knee had an itch," I say as the waitress continues toward her destination. I leave my pen on the ground.

LOW SEASON IN GRADO

Gary Singh

Before the high season
when the bandsaw chorus of German tourism
begins to slice through the simplicity,
this timeless island of Grado at the northern Adriatic fringe,
native nest of Biagio Marin, whose elementary verse
captured flowers in the lagoon, where winds cry of the
Virgin Mary, a perfect espresso writes me
a poem as a warm drizzle lays the backbeat for a symphony
of sleeping sailboats in the harbor.

A lifeless Austrian boat
teaches me about metaphors, a bare vessel
with flakes of rust floating in scattered pools
on the bow, sewing seeds to the glory of Habsburg,
a relic from absentee owners who left long ago,
$3800 Euros on its fading sign, for sale, curling at the
damp edges, while the Adriatic speaks of wars for men's
souls, the lives of fishermen, popes, patriarchs,
and the collapse of empires.

Only then does Biagio Marin
steer me into the present, along the road
to his abandoned home on Via Marchesini
where stems of ivy cover the gray facade like a road map,
where the solitude of this island village
echoes with the spirit of its favorite son, his mystical dialect
seeded from west and east, from Nietzsche and Tagore
to the migrant birds of today.

There in the silence
of my morning, as the drizzle gives way
to cosmic stretches of light and sun-soaked stones,
I realize the luxuries of business travel mean nothing
against dilated skies and red passionflowers,
my two-room suite means nothing to a family of sparrows outside
in the alcove, and when the season comes, German tourists
with their terrible coffee will pale by comparison to the
poetry of those who travel with Biagio Marin.

ONE, TWO, THREE, HIKE!

Lawrence Morgan

The evening before my assault on Rincon Peak found me stuffing my brand-new backpack full to the brim with a bold assortment of camping paraphernalia mail-ordered over the years, none of which had been used. No more armchair excursions for this buckaroo; I was ready for a real expedition!

After all, I was planning to spend the night outside.

I sat in the garage surrounded by a half-dozen first aid kits, four flashlights, two camp stoves, several nesting sets of pots and pans, water purification kits, an inflatable pillow, a solar shower, a handful of pocket knives festooned with miniature tools, and a nifty hodgepodge of survival blankets, mirrors, whistles, waterproof-matches, folding-shovels, fire-starter pastes, emergency strobe lights, candle lanterns and freeze-dried meals.

"Good thing I bought such a large backpack," I congratulated myself, cramming in another armful.

It seemed wise to add a few luxuries, like a flask of whiskey and a jar of salsa for the tortilla chips. The pack fairly bristled with goodies as it leaned against the wall. It looked like a great, green nylon sausage, near to bursting.

I lashed my sleeping bag to the top, my tent to the bottom, buckled my binoculars, camera, and sandals to the front, and tried to pick it up.

Nothing doing.

I scooted back down the wall, slipped my arms into the shoulder straps, leaned forward and forced my legs to slowly straighten. Connective tissue creaked and groaned, but held fast. I cinched the waist-strap tight and swayed out of the garage like a hunchbacked ape. My Sierra cup swung like a pendulum on its lanyard and cracked me above the eye.

Oh, wilderness!

I wrestled with a small problem at the crack of dawn next morning: how was I going to get my gear into the back of my three-cylinder Daihatsu Charade? I finally slung the backpack sideways with both arms and gave it a simultaneous, mighty Macarena shove with my hip. It brushed the lip of the trunk and landed with a thud on the folded-down back seat. The little car rocked on its springs, and I was off.

The trailhead was a forty-five-mile drive south and east of Tucson. One climbs Rincon Peak from the backside, as it were. The final leg was a rugged twenty-mile stretch of forbidding gravel road, which dead-ended at a grove of tall mesquite trees. Mine was the only car in sight. A narrow gate with a Forest Service sign on it heralded the beginning of the Rincon Peak Trail. The sign read: Steep, Difficult Terrain. Water Unreliable. Happy Valley Saddle 4.9 Miles. Rincon Peak 9.5 Miles.

I crept through the gate with the monster on my back and left civilization behind.

Thankfully I had purchased a trail-guide that offers fairly detailed information about the Rincon Peak Trail. I foolishly disregarded the section in the beginning which states: "…. extremely difficult trail, the most difficult in the entire Rincon Mountain Wilderness Area. Only to be attempted by expert hikers in peak physical condition…" etc., etc.

"Balderdash," I thought, skimming through that bit, and continued on my way.

The first mile or so was a pleasant, level walk along Miller Creek. There was abundant shade, and the desert was in bloom. I whistled and chirruped with the birds. I stumbled along gaily beneath my burden and twirled my walking stick like a baton. Life was dandy.

Then suddenly I was out of the shade and in the middle

of a vast field of sunbaked boulders the size of dumpsters. The creek vanished. Someone cruelly turned up the heat. The trail turned into a friable gravel rut eight inches wide by ten inches deep and commenced climbing relentlessly uphill.

The desert silence was profound, broken only by the distant hum of what I assumed were killer bees and my own labored breathing. The thought of rattlesnakes crossed my mind more than once. I paused to blow and rest my backpack on an outcropping of rock (a technique I mastered and perfected by midmorning) and glanced at the guidebook.

It said: "After a seemingly endless climb through boulder-strewn ravines and switchbacking around clumps of shadeless manzanita bushes the trail drops into an exceptionally pretty area..."

I struggled up another hundred feet of broken rock and wished desperately for the trail to "drop into an exceptionally pretty area." It did not. The "seemingly endless climb" section was remarkably accurate, however.

The view did gradually become extraordinary the higher I went, but it was difficult to appreciate through the torrents of sweat pouring down my face and the clouds of gnats that niggled at the corners of my eyes. By then I was climbing sometimes on all fours, and making pitiful, mewling noises in the back of my throat.

Every ten yards or so I stopped to rest and drink water in gulps, downing my supply at a dangerous rate. The terrain features I was most keen to observe were outcroppings of rock at the proper height for me to back up to and rest my pack upon.

I stopped for lunch at noon, having hiked unsteadily uphill for five hours that seemed like ten. A long, flat boulder under the shade of the first evergreen tree I'd seen welcomed me. I used a horizontal branch and a cunning system of carabineers and rope to suspend the backpack in mid-air, that being the only way I could take it off without rupturing a disc. I shrugged out of it, doing only minor damage to my back, and collapsed thankfully onto the boulder. The evil ripstop nylon sausage swung from the tree with silent malice.

Water was a problem. I had consumed three out of four quarts at that point, but the guidebook informed me that pools of fresh water were usually available at Happy Valley Saddle. I looked forward to using one of my purification kits for the first time.

Not that I had much faith in the book; I was still waiting for the trail to drop me off in Shangri-La, but I had little choice. I didn't have enough water left to go back down the mountain, and besides, something strange had happened to my legs. The chemicals that cause muscles to contract after extension had somehow leaked out of them. It wasn't automatic anymore. I couldn't trust my legs to take me downhill now; they were only trained to go up.

Then I heard voices! Intruders on my mountain! The place was so desolate, so remote...I never expected to see anyone else. I know now why hermits living alone in the woods hide from people. A person feels exposed and vulnerable in surroundings of such primal magnificence. It's hard to maintain emotional barriers in the wilderness. Your soul is open and other people can look right in.

I watched the bend in the trail and listened intently. I had barely negotiated that stretch thirty minutes before, wheezing and stumbling like a gut-shot elk. I pitied whoever was coming up that cursed hill. I'd been there.

And here they came, a group of four *elderly* people walking *briskly* up the hill toward me. Their leader was a lady of seventy-five or eighty, leathery and spare. She wasn't sweating; she wasn't even breathing hard. She wore a huge straw hat, and a pair of water bottles were strapped like six-guns to her waist. Slung low rather daringly, I thought with uncharacteristic venom. She clutched a thick "Field guide to Desert Flowers" in one liver-spotted hand, and in the other brandished a carved walking stick decorated with shells and feathers.

She raised her stick in the air like a wagon-train scout and the procession halted before me. Her three companions took meager sips from their water bottles and stared at me. The leader didn't even deign to drink.

I was very conscious of my sweat-stained shirt, my grimy face, my blistered feet that looked like pot-roast.

"Good morning," she said.

I nodded pleasantly, still out of breath.

"Lovely day for a walk. We're going up to Happy Valley for the afternoon to look at flowers."

My mouth fell open. For the afternoon! I wasn't even certain that I'd get to Happy Valley, let alone by afternoon.

I smiled noncommittally and pointed to my pack. "Hunnert pounds easy," I wheezed. "Plan to stay out maybe a month or two."

The other three lost interest in me and examined the surrounding vegetation with keen eyes, pointing out little blossoms to one another. They exchanged Latin names and thumbed through the illustrations in their field guides.

The leader looked at me doubtfully. "Oh well," she said, "we want to be back at the parking lot by sunset. Enjoy your stay."

I smiled and waggled my fingers at them as they left. They snaked up the hill at a rate of speed that left me cringing on my boulder. I forced myself into the harness and staggered after them, determined to advance at least another hundred yards before they came galloping back at the end of the day.

The trail worsened and became steeper. Not falling down became the focal point of my hiking technique. After a grueling two hours I crested the shoulder of the mountain, and sure enough, the trail dropped into an area of exceptional beauty.

A deep ravine was on my right, and wild grapevines trailed gracefully from Ponderosa pines on the slope to my left into its depth. They covered the path with dappled shade, and with cracked lips, I kissed the cover of my guidebook. A small creek ran through the bottom of the ravine, and for a short time, the trail led me downhill toward it. I wasn't exactly walking at that point; I was sort of lurching forward in short spurts on columns of rubber, but downhill all the same.

After the sudden coolness and striking loveliness of the ravine, the trail made a sharp uphill swing for a half-mile. I glared at the slope and gritted my teeth. I trudged along in a stupor, reciting nonsense rhymes in time to my walk.

At five in the evening, a bend in the trail brought me into Happy Valley at last, elevation 6200 feet. The valley was filled with giant Ponderosa pines, sixty to eighty feet tall. The ground was carpeted six inches deep with fallen needles; my footsteps were muffled as I walked. The temperature dropped to seventy-five degrees in the shade, and the gnarled, granite forehead of Rincon Peak was visible about four miles away. I had made it! I was tempted to dance a little jig, but my quivering limbs ridiculed the thought.

I followed the trail another mile or so into the forest and selected a campsite on a bluff overlooking a trickle of water that disappeared and reappeared along a green belt of dense moss and rocks.

I suspended my backpack from a tree and set about making camp. By dusk, the tent was up, and a fire crackled in a Forest Service fire-pit that looked as though it hadn't been used in a very long time. I poured a tall whiskey into a short plastic glass and watched the evening fuse to night.

The night was very quiet. The forest was very dark. I was very alone. I put some water on to boil; the clatter of pots and pans reassured me. I hummed; I looked noisily through my gear. I didn't know what to do with myself. The silence was huge. I thought about bears.

Bears! I added wood to the fire. The flames licked at the night and cast flickering, ursine shadows in the near distance. The aroma of freeze-dried lasagna wafted through the clean air. I recalled reading something about a bear's sense of smell being ten thousand times more acute than a man's.

Odd rustlings in the undergrowth fractured the silence. I poured another drink. I looked at the limbs of the tree above me and calculated how long it would take to climb. I remembered that black bears can climb extremely well...

I dug out my harmonica and played as loudly as I could, wailing the anti-bear blues into the night. I hobbled in a primitive, shuffling dance around my fire. I whooped and hollered, and turned on all my flashlights. Their crisscrossed beams stabbed the darkness, but the edge of the forest was blacker than ever. I ate the spaceman lasagna in an atavistic state of panic and chased it down with whiskey. That seemed to help. I poured another and carried my leftovers a few dozen yards away from camp as a decoy.

I returned to the fire and polished off the flask, the fear of bears transformed into tipsy arrogance. After one last howl at the moon, I crawled into the tent and slept like a dead man until dawn.

When I woke up the only muscles functioning were the ones governing my eyelids. All the others had metamorphosed into lumps of tortured tissue; there wasn't a spark of electricity among them. I could tell I was lying on my back, but only because a pinecone was wedged under my spine. I resigned myself to starve to death on the mountain because I couldn't make myself get out of bed. My head felt like a cracked clay pot.

I looked at the tent door flap and noted I hadn't fully closed the zipper the night before. A giant wasp with hairy legs and a two-inch stinger flew straight through the gap and hurtled toward my face. I learned later this was a tarantula hawk, but at the time it looked like some hideous being from the Inferno, and I made a noise like a stepped-on chicken.

Amazing what adrenaline can do for a person! I was on my feet and outside the tent, stark naked, in less than a second. The sun was just peeking over the eastern shoulder of the mountain, and I was a physical wreck.

I required more than rest and recuperation; I needed a whole new body. I was amazed at the depth of my exhaustion and daydreamed about pools of Ben-Gay.

After a prodigious breakfast (anything to reduce the weight I was doomed to carry), I fussed around camp. I showered with the solar shower, filled all the canteens, and attempted a few agonizing stretching exercises. I limped through the trees and glades nearby and kept an eye out for bear sign.

Mostly, though, I listened to the wild silence, a profound silence with so many parts it defied dissection. There were liquid bird melodies, the staccato jackhammer of a woodpecker on a dead tree, the abrupt explosion of a pine cone dropping through the canopy sixty feet above, the soft hum of billions of insects like the sound of a muted, distant generator. I heard the silver gurgle of the stream sliding over a mossy ledge and bubbling across rounded stones, the excited chatter of a gray squirrel upside down on a tree trunk, the rustle of a lizard darting through the bushes.

And there was the wind, the varying, faraway rush of the wind. I heard the wind always, mostly in the tops of the tallest Ponderosas, but sometimes a spiral summer breeze would rise from the desert flatlands below and advance like an infant tornado into the foothills. I could hear it progress up the mountain and into the valleys of the high country as it swirled closer and closer. I watched it bend the treetops as it rushed past on its urgent errand, showering my camp with pine needles and motes of dust.

I hoisted the devil pack onto my back and headed down the mountain, thankful for the assistance of gravity. I slid and scrambled down the trail, telling myself a dozen times I'd never go backpacking again. I longed for my armchair and my mail-order catalogs.

I cursed my pack, the sharp gravel in my boots, my derelict limbs who anointed me afresh with aches and pains, but I saw things more clearly somehow. I looked with a certain fondness at places in the trail that had nearly destroyed me the day before. I know I'll go back to that magical place one day. I left something there, or perhaps I found something.

UBIQUITOUS
Thomas Piekarski

Before we give in to isolation,
let our shadows drag us under the waves,
make a pact with desolation
that we'll eventually change our ways,
instead step back and observe the universe
in reverse the way it was made.
Then cast aside revisions of pride
given up to uproarious plunder.

Look under the rocks where lizards hide,
peer up to the sky and ponder what wonders
lie ahead. Cry to the almighty gods thrown
off their thrones, Osiris, Thor, Zeus, Jesus,
Allah, Buddha and the rest. They all meant
some sort of good in their respective sects.

Restore them to their rightful stature,
for they all embody ubiquitous Nature.

TURKISH APPLE HARVEST
Dave Gregory

One apple goes up, two come down. The movement catches my eye.

A curious outsider, an aimless tourist meandering across the Anatolian plain, I approach the tiny orchard. A young boy with short dark hair looks about seven as he stands beneath a small tree laden with crimson fruit. Despite the heat and rough terrain, he wears stiff black dress shoes and grey socks. Beige pants don't quite reach his ankles. A worn but clean white knitted vest covers his plaid collared shirt. Holding an apple in one hand, he aims, lobs it straight up, then steps back as it disappears in the foliage. Two red orbs come thudding down.

Nearby, a brown donkey with tall, twitching ears is hitched to an unpainted wooden cart. A young girl, his sister perhaps, sits in front, her legs dangling behind the stationary animal. She looks about ten. A peach scarf covers her hair and shoulders. A white sweater is buttoned over a long, faded, blue print dress.

Collecting both apples, the boy hands one to the girl who places it behind her on the cart. He tosses the second into the lower branches and steps out of the way. One apple comes down heavily bruised, another only slightly.

I can't help laughing at the inefficiency.

Both children turn and see me for the first time. They appear startled. I feel ashamed for disturbing this serene and bucolic tableau; wealth and privilege give me no right to pass judgment.

The girl speaks softly to her brother who shrugs, dismissing me, before handing her more fallen fruit.

The hiking trail bends toward the children before veering

away. Stepping closer, I count fifteen apples in the cart. The boy continues tossing the battered apple, missing sometimes but more often dislodging a fleshy reward, which he makes no attempt to catch.

The girl turns again to see whether I've gone. My presence must be unnerving, but I want to help.

"You've got to shake it," I say.

The boy stares, uncomprehending.

I mime jostling the trunk with bare hands.

A hint of fear crosses his face.

"Shake the tree," I ineptly explain. Mimicking a tight hold, forcefully agitating the wood, a breathy: "aahh-aahh-aahh-aahh" escapes my lungs.

The boy edges closer to his big sister, almost hiding behind the cart.

I realize it might look like I'm strangling someone.

"I'll show you," I say and climb the tree. It separates into three large boughs. "Like this," I exclaim, wrapping my hands round a wide branch. Throttling it, I hope the boy recognizes my earlier gesture.

Limbs creak, leaves swish and fall. One apple lands with a thud. Inspired, I thrash harder. Dozens of succulent crimson orbs release and gravity takes over. I stop, smell bark on my hands, then turn and grab the next branch. More leaves rustle as apples pound out a reassuring drumbeat. Through twigs and greenery, I see the boy's face, eyes wide with wonder as delicious fruit falls like rain. His joy is palpable.

I shake the last large branch, then jump down, careful not to tread on apples carpeting the stony, weedy ground. "Is that enough?" I ask.

He doesn't reply, but how can he not be impressed? I expect a smile or a handshake. Maybe his sister will offer an apple with gratitude.

Seconds pass. Anything could happen. They might even

invite me to feast with their parents, where they'll breathlessly recount my miraculous feat.

But no. In silence, the boy raises an imploring arm and points to the next tree.

I laugh louder than before. "You greedy little shit," I exclaim, knowing he won't understand.

Still laughing, I wipe sweat from my brow. Inhaling sweet-scented air, I climb the suggested tree and recall my infant nephew flinging a plastic cup from his high chair to the floor. Each time my brother retrieved it, he tossed it again. This went on until my sister-in-law entered and explained: "He's experimenting with power. He's throwing to *make you* bring it back. This can go on all day."

Thankfully, the Turkish boy doesn't make me climb a third tree. I wave and he watches me depart. His sister never makes eye contact.

Following the path, I watch cloud shadows race across this bizarre Cappadocian landscape. Over the millennia, volcanic ash compacted into water-soluble rock prone to erosion. Beneath random granite slabs on the surface, tall cones and chimneys were coaxed from the porous earth as it gradually wore away under heavy rain and lashing wind.

An improbable skyline of chalky pinnacles rises high above the plain. I wonder what it's like living behind those rough-hewn doorways, courtyards, and windows in a complicated warren of above-ground caves and tunnels dug centuries earlier.

Local topsoil is another geological miracle. Neat rows of fat zucchinis and orange peppers flourish alongside bulbous red tomatoes. Clusters of pale green grapes grow lazily on the ground, spilling over parched soil rather than hanging from vines.

From the valley edge, the trail zigzags up a gentle slope of powdery rock. The donkey returns to view and I hear the boy and girl arguing—she refuses to allow more apples in the cart, even though it's nowhere near full. I assume "yeterli" is the Turkish word for "enough." She repeats this while blocking his every effort.

Losing patience, she prods the donkey with a stick. It brays and lurches forward, leaving her brother behind. He curses, tears off his vest, then flings it at his feet. Crouching, he fills it with every remaining apple. Knitted fabric stretches and bulges. The improvised bag resembles a heavy sack of potatoes, enormous against his tiny hands and thin arms. Straining to lift, a single fruit tumbles out. He drops the entire load, shoves the stray apple back in and rises again.

Regret washes over me. Instead of a wise traveler who saved an innocent boy some time, I'm the snake who inflamed his greed. Full of shame, I slither away.

ARMISTICE DAY
Dan Morey

I met him at a restaurant on the outskirts of Saint-Avold. We sat in a windowless dining room, enclosed by mirrored walls.

"You look hideous," I said. "Where did you find such an awful sweater?"

"It was a birthday present," he said.

"A present? From what mortal enemy?"

"You."

I took a quaff of my Manhattan. "Well, I can't say I'm surprised. But why in the world, dear brother, would you wear it?"

The waiter cleared his throat. He'd been standing beside the table, grinning like an imbecile.

"What do you want?" I said.

"Your order, monsieur."

"Don't monsieur me. We're American. Bring us steaks. Medium rare."

My brother gulped his martini and waved the empty glass at the waiter. He'd aged considerably since our last meeting; his face was sallow and wrinkled, like a golden raisin.

"How did you get so old and so ugly so fast?" I said. "Last year you looked almost human."

"At least I'm not fat."

"This is my winter weight. I put it on to keep warm. By June I'll look like Johnny Weissmuller in his prime."

"Johnny Weissmuller wasn't bald."

"Neither am I."

We were the only customers in the restaurant. A decade ago it had been one of the best in northern France. Packed tables.

Merry conversation. Bright, clean surfaces. Now everything white had gone slightly yellow: the ceiling, the tablecloths, the waiters' jackets.

"I don't want steak," said my brother.

"Excuse me?"

"I don't want steak. I want lobster."

"Well, why didn't you say something?"

When I told the waiter to change the order, he informed me that the steak was already being cooked.

"Good. Feed it to the rats," I said.

He slunk off, and my brother chortled. I looked in the mirror at the back of his head. Thick, gray hair. Not a hint of scalp. Bastard.

We drank without speaking. I could hear thelow rumble of a television in the bar, some pots clanging in the kitchen, the faint pitter-patter of rain on the roof.

A woman entered and sat at a table in the corner. She was wearing a green dress with a felt hat and fox stole. On her chest, over her heart, was a blue cornflower—the Bleuet de France—commemorating Armistice Day.

"How old do you think she is?" said my brother.

"She's got a dead animal around her neck, so pretty old."

"As old as we are?"

"As old as you are."

The waiter brought the woman a drink on a tray. She said, "Merci," and lit a cigarette.

"Redhead," I said. "With very good posture."

The woman turned. "Are you gentlemen discussing me?"

"You speak English," said my brother.

"And your accent isn't completely unbearable," I said.

"Nice of you to say so." She took a drag on her cigarette then held it off to the side with a cocked wrist. The smoke drifted up in velvety curls. I wondered why she wasn't wearing gloves. They were the only thing missing.

"We're on our way to the American Cemetery," said my brother.

"Veterans?"

"Good God, no," I said. "We're visiting our father's grave. We meet here every year on November eleventh."

"Even though we never knew him," said my brother.

"We were toddlers when he died. Fighting to save you people from the Krauts. We had a tough childhood thanks to Herr Hitler."

"France is in your debt," she said, returning to her cigarette.

The scent of tobacco aroused old cravings. I could remember my last B&H vividly. I'd smoked it halfway, then used the rest to burn my Actors' Equity card. The transition from leading man to character actor was not for me.

The waiter served our food. My steak was overdone. He took it away and brought another, probably the one I'd sent to the rats. "I'll eat it, but I'm not going to pay for it," I told my brother. He wheezed with delight. "Do you ever?"

I had another Manhattan to help choke the meat down. The woman was on her second brandy and a third cigarette.

"Excuse me," I said.

She turned. "Yes?"

"If you had to sleep with one of us, which one would it be?"

My brother burst out laughing and sprayed gin everywhere. He'd been a big tippler in his day, but couldn't hold his liquor anymore. The woman didn't seem shocked at all.

"The one with the hair," she said.

Of course. He'd always been considered handsome. A pilot for TWA. The idol of every dopey stewardess. "Are you sure?" he said. "Baldy here once played Hamlet."

"I would've guessed Falstaff," she said, glancing at my midsection.

My brother stumbled over to the woman with his lobster. "You're my kinda gal! Have some shellfish!"

He settled in beside her, leaving me alone at the table, surrounded by mirrors. Everywhere I looked I saw myself. From the side, receding hairline. From the front, creased brow and blotchy skin. I thought of my father, decomposing under French dirt all these years.

"Waiter!" I said.

He approached slowly, with a stooped gait, as if he was afraid I might belt him.

"I can't finish this steak. It's as dry as the damned Sahara. Bring me another."

He took the plate back to the kitchen. The woman met my eyes in the mirror and said, "Difficult people die alone." Then shelooked away, leaving me to stare at my reflection.

Later, in the cemetery, my brother fell beside our father's grave, smashing a bottle of cognac.

"Get up, you oaf," I said.

He lay there, blubbering. "My heart's shot. The doc told me I could go anytime. Hey. I love that woman in the restaurant. I really do. Do you think she'd marry me? It's not too late, is it? I don't want to die alone."

"Everyone dies alone," I said.

As we walked back to the car through the rows of pale crosses, I wondered, as I did every year, if it would be our final trip.

OH, PARDON
Matthew Menary

My first trip overseas I decided to waste on Paris. Waste, knowing full well that on a seven-day, six-night excursion, I would not even scratch the surface of the surface. Of course, it was not wasted. For Paris, even the surface of the surface is worth it. I went back again and again.

The first time for most things is when mistakes are made, and not just mistakes tied to the event, but mistakes easily avoided as they do not relate to anything new. Travel, being unfamiliar ground to me, was loaded with pitfalls even for very short trips. For example, away games were a distraction to me when I was on my high school wrestling team. My second wrestling bout was an away match forty minutes from my school, not so far geographically, but a journey across cultural lines. When our bus pulled into the cross-town school, all I could do was stare at the strange building, the other-worldly gym with foreign-looking orange and black banners, and the poorly-lit locker room. My opponent, my age, from a different culture, in a different shade of skin, was a most gracious and serious opponent. Strong and athletic, but smooth and soft under my martial grip, he mostly exchanged equal holds with me, neither of us making much progress through the first period. By the second, I knew his moves and I also knew he was more skilled than I was, and that it was only a matter of time before I would be pinned, probably in the third period if not by the end of the second. I should have fought harder, but in an already strange situation, I had the irresistible impulse to see if I knew his next move, if I had him figured out. I just had to know, so I waited. I was right. I was also pinned. The coach was not happy, but he would have been livid if he knew where my focus had been. Foreignness was a distraction that opened the door to an impulse that turned me off the path of my original intention.

Paris—the city of light, the city of food, the city of beauty—was a distraction. On my first visit, I was ripe for an impulse, but on my guard, too. Not knowing the language tamped down my adventurousness, and there were too many things to do— les Champs-Élysées, le Musée Picasso, le Louvre. Trouble was the last thing on my mind. I was too busy.

I was busy, yes, and in a hurry, too. The metro solved most of my travel problems. Bright, crowded, and humming with moving trains, it was like a city in itself. With the simplicity and ease I had in getting around, I did not wonder that the metro was so well used, with people everywhere. I should have paid more attention when, almost magically, I found myself quite alone walking down a long, brightly lit corridor. It was silent, too, but I didn't notice how lonely and quiet it was. My mind was on my next destination.

As I turned right, I saw, at the end of a long walkway, a man standing with a white cane, holding a small white Styrofoam cup. *Oh, he's blind. I can give him some money*, I thought. *That will be easy and a good way to give back to this wonderful city.*

I started to dig in my pocket for a heavy ten-franc coin as each step brought me closer. Then I wondered what I would say, and then how I would say it. *Here you are, sir*, I thought to say. *But how? "Voici, Monsieur." Here what? "Voici, Monsieur, un coin." Is it un coin or une coin? Le coin?*

I came closer still. I thought maybe I would just play it safe and pass by. *He's fine. He is shabby-looking but probably dresses that way for effect. I bet he has more in the bank than I do.* My mind raced. *No*, I thought, *I will just go on my way. I won't need to figure out if coin is masculine or feminine. I won't have to butcher Monsieur— one of the easiest words in French, one of the*

first words you learn— with my fat, maladroit, American tongue.
No, I'll just get to where I am going, no need to embarrass myself.

Only feet from him, the impulse hit. I thought, *I'll just give him the coin*, and I dropped it into his cup with a clank as my coin hit the coins already there.

Of course, in the silent walkway and with my comfortable, soft-soled walking shoes, this blind man had no idea anyone was there. The disjointed monologue going on in my head was so deafening to me, it made me lose track of the silence and the fact that the man was blind. When the coin clanked into his cup, his shoulders went up and he let out a cry, followed by a stream of words in French that I needed no dictionary to translate.

YOU TURNED TWENTY-FIVE IN EURODISNEY

Matt Mason

Like in a fairy tale, there was a magic gift
(a bank's random drawing) and there was love,

the memories, though, the details
are as gone now as the dress from a fairy godmother when
11:59 ticks to 12

without clock chimes, just digital silence,
a few thousand midnights
each taking a thread
away.

At most, there's one glass slipper left
among mice and pumpkins and torn, old things,

you mainly remember her,
a breakfast where Goofy toppled comically,
a cake of indeterminate flavor,
twenty-five candles in it.

What sticks
is how much is missing.
Even this person you loved so much.

When there's not
enough magic,
you both know, to make what doesn't fit

fit,
you have to show patience, have to know
you don't break up in Disneyland
you wait, like a script,

for a dark hotel room out in Paris,
calm conversation,
then a flight alone,
airplane seat tray table

you will watch
like a TV screen gone static which you're too tired to change
for hour after hour

half
your life
ago.

A CONVERSATION WITH TIMOTHY J. LOCKHART

Lowestoft Chronicle

Timothy J. Lockhart
(Photography: Margaret E.G. Lockhart)

Crime writer Timothy J. Lockhart, a Former U.S. Navy intelligence officer and retired Navy Reserve captain who now works a lawyer in Virginia, has published many articles and book reviews in a variety of publications, most notably *The Virginian-Pilot*. In 2017, his debut novel, a suspense thriller titled *Smith*, garnered strong critical reviews, with *Booklist* remarking on the "beautifully wrought scenes" and "artfully done violence." His subsequent book, *Pirates*, published this past April by Stark House Press, is a modern-day high-seas thriller that is set in the hazardous rough waters of the Caribbean. Another standalone novel with a tough, ex-military central character, *Pirates* has the same taut, suspenseful prose and disturbing blend of violence and eroticism that helped make *Smith* a critical success.

Here, in an exclusive interview with *Lowestoft Chronicle*, Lockhart discusses his novels, his literary influences, and his writing process.

Lowestoft Chronicle (LC): Your debut novel, *Smith*, received positive reviews and was praised in *Booklist* for its "beautifully wrought scenes" and "artfully done violence." What's the backstory on the novel? When did you begin this novel and how long did it take to write?

Timothy J. Lockhart (TJL): I began the novel in 2013, and, while working full time as a lawyer, it took me two years to write and polish the manuscript.

I started with the character Smith and the bare bones of a plot and then added other characters and plot events as I went along. I worked without an outline and didn't know how the story would end until I ended it.

LC: Was this your first completed manuscript or had you been working on others prior to it?

TJL: *Smith* was the third novel I finished, but the first one I sold.

LC: How would you describe the experience of writing it?

TJL: It was fun actually. I didn't know where the story would ultimately go, so I kept surprising myself—and I hope that readers were surprised as they went through the novel.

LC: The resilient, hard-as-nails assassin, known only as Smith, is perhaps an unusual choice for a protagonist, especially for a debut author. How challenging was it writing the novel from a female's perspective? After all, this is a hardboiled tale with steamy scenes, graphic violence, and plenty of feminine introspection.

TJL: I served with quite a number of women in the Navy and had two female bosses (one a Navy admiral and one an Army colonel), so I like to think that I can represent the thinking of a female character, at least to some extent. I have some very helpful women readers who went through the draft manuscript and gave me some pointers. Getting comments on a draft from insightful—and candid—readers is always helpful, in my view.

LC: There's an interesting article in *The Washington Post* where you're quoted at length on the topic of the language of cops. You note that while some writers like Dashiell Hammett came to their knowledge of copspeak through "ride-alongs" with police to get the right flavor and dialogue for their books, probably most crime writers pick up the lingo through TV police dramas and movies and "crime or private eye novels by Elmore Leonard, Raymond Chandler and a host of others." How would you describe your own approach to writing dialogue? And did your work with the intelligence community help with the writing of *Smith*?

TJL: Yes, my intelligence background helped a lot, especially with the characters of the Director and the Assistant Director in *Smith*. I just try to write the way people actually talk, but of course, I leave out all the "ahs," "umms," and "you knows."

LC: Your latest novel, *Pirates*, is a blend of adventure fiction, thriller, and a modern-day interpretation of the swashbuckler. Here, though, Hal—the tough and courageous hero who saves and defends the beautiful damsel in distress against a dastardly villain—is a grotesquely disfigured, deeply troubled veteran who has withdrawn from society. Although skilled in combat, he's physically impaired, mentally scarred, and out-of-his-depth when it comes to intimacy. Interestingly, the novel is as much a romance as it is a thriller. Was that always your intention or did the story take a different course during the writing of it?

Was writing this novel a faster, smoother process than *Smith*?

TJL: I wrote a draft of *Pirates* before I wrote *Smith*, but after I sold *Smith* I went back the significantly reworked *Pirates*. The novelist Rick Ollerman gave me great advice about revising the beginning of the story, and Greg Shepard (my publisher) and an insightful reader friend named Warren Tisdale gave me great advice about revising the ending. So the as-published book is quite different (and, I hope, better) than the original manuscript.

LC: As was the case with Smith, the character Hal is a psychologically wounded former soldier who is given a new purpose in life. Both Hal and Smith are not so much seeking redemption as discovering how to love again and finding themselves in a situation where they must fight for others and their own survival. In the case of both of these novels, did the story or the characters develop first? How detailed were your outlines before you began work on these novels?

TJL: I started with the characters of Smith, Hal, and Ana in the two books. I had an outline for *Pirates* but ended up not following it much. I didn't use an outline for *Smith*, and I'm not using an outline for the novel I'm writing now. For me, it seems to work better just to jump off the diving board and see where and how I land.

LC: For many years, you've reviewed books of all different literary genres, and yet with your own fiction writing, it seems you favor crime fiction. Did you adapt your writing to appeal to this market to forge a literary career or do you most enjoy writing thrillers with hardboiled protagonists?

TJL: I write the kind of fiction I like to read: hardboiled crime fiction that breaks new ground—or at least tries to. I also enjoy reading nonfiction—mostly biography and history—but I haven't tried writing any yet although I do have a few ideas for nonfiction books.

LC: When did you actively start writing fiction for publication? Your story "Last Night at the Skipper's Lounge" appears in a 2017 issue of *Down & Out Magazine*. Is this a one-off short story or have you been writing others?

TJL: I'd written a couple of novels prior to *Smith*, and the process of writing and rewriting them was my apprenticeship, so to speak. *Smith* was the first novel I wrote with the definite goal of selling it, and that's how things turned out.

I'm primarily a novelist, not a short story writer. Rick Ollerman encouraged me to try a short story, and "Skipper's Lounge" was the result. I have ideas for other short stories and may get to some of them after I finish the new novel.

LC: Who would you credit as the writers who influenced you the most? I remember you once reviewing the work of Gil Brewer and speaking very highly of him. Would he be one of your key influences?

TJL: Gil Brewer, David Goodis, Hammett, Chandler, Cain, Elmore Leonard, the American Charles Williams, the early John D. MacDonald...I could go on and on. Any good fiction that I've read has influenced me in some way...often by making me wish I could write that well!

LC: You've written for numerous journals and newspapers over the decades and have been a correspondent for *The Virginian Pilot* for many years. How and when did you get involved in journalism? What was the first piece you had published?

TJL: I began writing for the school newspaper when I was about 12 years old and have been writing ever since. If I hadn't been first a Navy officer and then a lawyer, I probably would have gone into journalism. But I like the way things have worked out—I've been very lucky.

LC: Are you currently working on a new manuscript, and will you continue to focus on suspenseful thrillers?

TJL: Yes, and yes. I've finished two more novels in draft and am now polishing them for publication. And I have a fifth novel underway. So stand by for more thrills and chills to come!

HSI-WEI'S VISIT TO KO QING-ZHAO

Robert Wexelblatt

The poet Chen Hsi-wei and the landscape painter Ko Qing-zhao had not seen one another in two years. During that time, three letters from Hsi-wei had reached Ko; but, owing to the poet's nomadic life, the painter had nowhere he could address a reply. The one he tried to send through a mutual friend in Daxing chased the poet around Emperor Wen's dominions in vain.

The two men had one of those friendships that are struck up in an hour and outlast even long separations. As is usual when two people instantly take to one another, their liking was initially physical. Hsi-wei and Ko detected in one another's faces intelligence, sensibility, and honesty. Their immediate sympathy was deepened by the esteem in which each held the other's art. As they tilled different fields, their friendship was free of any taint of competition or jealousy. They were perceptive about one another's work, understood their aims, rejoiced in their achievements and growing reputations. Whenever one heard the other's name mentioned approvingly, he felt gratification.

While the vagabond Hsi-wei was always in motion and his livelihood insecure, Ko was settled quietly in Hsuan where he held a minor sinecure in the office of the magistrate. His income was not handsome but adequate for a bachelor whose major expenses were for artist's materials. Moreover, his job was not demanding and left Ko plenty of time for his real work, though less than he would have liked. Gradually, collectors began to seek him out and, when the peers of the great Zhan Ziqian were listed, Ko's name was frequently mentioned. As a young man, Ko saw Zhan's *Spring Excursion* and dedicated himself to the art of *Shan Shui*, mountain/water landscapes. This kind of painting does not aim at realistic representation but conveying the feelings aroused in the artist by the scenery. In Ko's landscapes, Nature is always still; even his waterfalls appear motionless. Movement is confined to the few human figures—tiny sages climbing with staffs, minuscule fisherman pulling up nets, drovers with miniature oxen. The busyness of these humans is too small to affect the tranquility of mountains and rivers. In this way, *Shan Shui* painting sets the colossal extent of the cosmos and the immeasurable length of history against the paltry exertions of humans.

Ko had labored hard to become a *Shan Shui* master. Had he been more ambitious and less attached to Hsuan, he might have aspired to and secured a position at court.

Hsi-wei's journey took him by slow-flowing rivers, through the forests and mountain passes of Huangshan. It was natural to think of himself as one of those little figures in his friend's landscapes, coming from nowhere, passing into oblivion. Yet the poet's spirits were high; the splendor of the scenery and the crispness of the air exhilarated him, honing the edge of his eagerness to see his friend.

Hsi-wei arrived in Hsuan at mid-morning, earlier than he had expected thanks to a peasant's offer of a ride on his oxcart. Hsi-wei took his ease atop fragrant radishes, carrots, and spring onions. As they descended toward the town, the air grew sultry, shapes dissolved, and there were clouds of insects. Hsi-wei began to miss the sweet air of the mountains, the noise of flowing rivers.

When they reached the market square, the poet helped the peasant set his crops out for sale. Bowing deeply, he thanked the good man for his kindness. Across the road, he spied a passing official in a high hat and ran up to ask the way to the magistrate's office.

The youthful official, who was trying to grow a beard without much success, took in Hsi-wei's dusty clothes and pack. He pointed and answered curtly. "Go that way and look for a red roof."

A guard lounged in the gateway of a low building with a steep red-tiled roof.

"You have business?" asked the guard in a tone both bored and surly.

Hsi-wei knew how to deal with such people.

"Yes, Your Honor," he said with a medium-sized bow. "I have business with Master Ko Qing-zhao."

The guard made a face. "You're in luck. He happens to be here, which he often isn't." He escorted Hsi-wei through the gate and pointed him down one of four corridors.

At the end of the hallway, Hsi-wei came to a small, windowless chamber. Here he found Ko Qing-zhao crouched at a low desk, brush in hand, a scroll open before him. There were scrolls everywhere, both big and little.

His old friend looked up, shouted, got to his feet. The two embraced. Bubbling over with pleasure, both spoke greetings at once, then burst out laughing.

"You inconsiderate peasant! Not a word of warning. Ah, what a wonderful surprise!"

"Well, I missed you. And I want to see what you're up to. Your work."

"I've seen three of your poems. People copy them, you know, and they make the rounds."

"Still unmarried?"

"Still making straw sandals?"

Hsi-wei shrugged. "We both have to eat," he said, gesturing toward the low desk, the inkpot. the scrolls."

"Just so. But I'll have you know I sold two pictures last month." It was a proof of their friendship that Ko did not try to conceal his pride.

"I'm not surprised. I've heard your name mentioned in the same sentence as Master Zhan Ziqian's. More than once."

Ko blushed. "Truly? Famous, am I? Like you?"

Hsi-wei scoffed, blushed, and again the two laughed.

"You must be starved," said Ko. "Let's get some rice and dumplings in the market then go to my place and talk and talk."

"What of all this?"

"What? This copying? It'll keep. Come, let's eat and then I'll show you my real work."

As they strolled to the marketplace, the friends summed up their lives since they had last met. At first, each felt there was far too much to tell but then found there was not. Ko said he copied documents, took down the testimony of witnesses, and painted his pictures. Hsi-wei said he traveled, met all sorts of people, made sandals out of straw and poems out of words. Though one was always on the move and the other planted fast in Hsuan, it seemed to them both that their outer lives had settled into routines. As for their inner lives, these could hardly be described quickly in the marketplace over dumplings and rice.

"Now," said Ko as they finished their meal, "we'll go to my place. It's not quite finished, but I want you to see my new picture."

"Is it a big one?"

"Huge, like its subject. *Autumn in the Yellow Mountains.* I'm putting everything into it."

As they walked toward the western edge of Hsuan, Ko fell silent. When Hsi-wei inquired if something were disturbing him, Ko replied that a troubling case was to come before the magistrate that week. Though it would involve personal risk, he said he felt compelled to intervene.

"And that would be dangerous for you?"

"The contestants are wealthy landlords with few scruples."

"I see."

"More to the point, as an official in the magistrate's office, I have no standing to participate. Even asking to do so would be deemed improper. I could lose my post."

"And yet you see a likely injustice?"

"That's it exactly."

"I want to hear all about the case. But only after I've seen your autumn painting."

Ko lived in a rambling old farmhouse. Ko explained that it had once been at the center of wide fields but had been overtaken by the town's expansion. Yet the building stood on what was still a considerable plot of land, some of which was cultivated. There were five fruit trees and a small but attractive stand of white pines. Ko had a lease on two rooms and also a long, narrow outbuilding by the pines which served as his studio.

Ko's painting was indeed large. It leaned against the shed's wall, matching its length and nearly its height. If Hsi-wei had seen Zhan's *Spring Excursion*, he would have recognized the work as both an homage and a sequel. The composition closely echoed Zhan's. A broad stretch of river runs diagonally from the top left to lower right. The stillness of the river is magically emphasized by many fine black lines. A white sampan with a standing boatman floats in the middle of the river at the very center of the picture. To the left juts a triangle of riverbank on which sit two female figures almost hidden by elms and pines. Where it is free of fallen leaves and pine straw, the ground is invitingly mossy. On the right of the picture, the opposite bank rises steeply to rocky hills behind which the Yellow Mountains extend in ever more misty waves to an empty background. Nothing of the sky to be seen, as in a map.

Hsi-wei was immediately attracted by the size and beauty of the picture. After taking in the whole, he stood close to examine its details. He felt he could hear the sound of the river in the delicate pattern of water lines. He took note of Ko's cleverness about the crookedness of the branches, was delighted to make out the nearly invisible pair of red footbridges below the water falling from the sheer rock faces. A minuscule peasant on his donkey and a brace of doves high in the branches of a pine were charming touches.

All the while, Ko was trying to look through his friend's eyes; he wanted to direct them to this or that patch of the painting. But there was no need, as Hsi-wei missed nothing, nor did the poet have to pretend to praise the work. He was astonished by how far Ko had advanced in his technique and full of admiration for such a large work, one fit for an imperial palace. Yet he said nothing until Ko begged for his reaction.

"It gives me two feelings."

"Yes?"

"The gladness and also the melancholy of—"

Ko finished the sentence with pleasure. "Of autumn," he said.

"Yes, autumn's just like this, or it ought to be. You've chosen the perfect moment, with the leaves in color and the air clear of humidity, bracing rather than cold." Hsi-wei stood back, looking from right to left, up to down. "It's splendid. But. . ."

"But?"

"But how will you ever outdo it?"

Ko laughed with gratification and relief.

The afternoon being fine, the two men took tea outside. Hsi-wei told Ko about a few of his adventures and showed him the poems they had provoked. Ko was bound to praise them, of course; but he did so sincerely and with insight. Yet Hsi-wei grew impatient and said he was eager to hear about the case that was troubling his friend.

"What's it about?"

"It has to do a large piece of land ten *li* to the west. Chin, the landlord, was an exceedingly good but unfortunate man.

He took his wife and son to see the work on the Grand Canal. They hired a boat. A sudden storm overturned the boat, and only Chin survived. He was a broken man but still a good one, perhaps even a better one.

"Chin died unexpectedly two months ago. The two neighboring landowners, Cao and Lu, who are quite unlike the virtuous Chin, both filed claims saying that he had left his land to them. However, I heard a different story from a friend of mine. According to him, Shao-sing, Chin's oldest servant, visited the inn and drank too many toasts to his deceased master. In his cups, he said that, shortly before his death, Chin invited Cao and Lu to dinner and informed them that, when his time came, he meant to leave his land to his tenants. Evidently, he died before drawing up a will to that effect. At least none has been found."

"I see."

"It gets more complicated. In fact, there are two wills. Cao and Lu both submitted wills in their favor, claiming they were written by Mr. Chin. Both have also produced witnesses, former servants in the Chin household. I believe the witnesses were bribed and both wills forged."

"Well, at least one must be. Why do you say both?"

"Because I think I know who forged them."

"And can this forger be produced in court?"

"Well," said Ko slowly, "that's unlikely. You see, I'm almost certain the work was done by Ouyang Xun, a calligrapher. Though we were not close friends I knew him well enough. He's a learned young man, a good doctor as well as an exceptional calligrapher. He lacks connections and his parents left him nothing. He was unhappy here in Hsuan, desperate to get away to the provincial capital where his talents would be better appreciated and rewarded. Shortly before the false wills were submitted, he paid me a farewell visit. He said that he'd come into some funds and would be leaving for the capital the next day. If I'm right, the last thing Xun would want is to return here."

Hsi-wei made up a proverb. "Liars don't always lie, just as honest men don't always tell the truth. Do you think this Xun would lie about the forgeries?"

"What can you mean? Forgeries *are* lies."

"Quite true, but not quite *his* lies."

"Ah, I see what you mean."

"Might a sworn statement from Xun be secured, perhaps by someone he knows and respects?"

"It's not impossible. He is not really a bad man."

"Could you yourself go to the capital and try to obtain such a statement?"

"Even if I succeeded, it would take a week and the hearing is in two days."

"Can the hearing be delayed?"

"Someone would have to come forward with a good reason for such a request."

"The old servant?"

"Shao-sing? He's frail and his position is insecure. He is likely to be dependent on either Cao or Lu. I think he'd be too frightened to speak up. Besides, even if he's suspicious of Cao and Lu, our good but prudent magistrate is unlikely to take the word of a servant over that of two powerful landowners."

Hsi-wei slapped his thigh. "Very well. I understand. You can't argue the case and the old servant won't request a delay. However, I can think of one person who is willing to do both."

Ko smiled. "You mean yourself?"

Hsi-wei, the peasant who was also a poet, the poet who was also a peasant, grinned.

"Are you willing to try?" he asked Ko.

"Without you, no. With you, yes."

When Ko asked how he planned to identify himself to the magistrate, Hsi-wei insisted he would say nothing that was untrue. "I'll say I'm a traveler who has heard of the perplexing Chin case and may be able to produce evidence that would resolve it. Then I'll say that this will require a week's delay. I suspect your magistrate will be eager to grant it."

"In that case," said Ko, "we'll have to dress you properly, in an official's robe. I can borrow one. Our magistrate is a decent and fair man, but he's insecure and has an irrational fear of other officials."

Ko arranged for Hsi-wei to meet with the magistrate who greeted the poet courteously. Just as Hsi-wei had guessed, the man was only too willing to have the case resolved in a way that would relieve him of a difficult decision, one that could make him a powerful enemy. He did not hesitate to grant the delay.

Ko requested leave to visit a sick uncle in the nearby village of Yagong but, before he left for the capital, the two friends paid a visit to Shao-sing, the old servant who had overheard what his master said at the dinner with Cao and Lu. The other Chin servants had returned to their families or found new jobs, but the faithful Shao-sing had appointed himself caretaker of the villa. He was still hale enough to sweep the rooms every day and see to the vegetable garden, which is where the two friends found him.

When Hsi-wei asked if he would be willing to testify, the old man shook his head.

"I wouldn't dare to do such a thing. I'm over sixty and I've never had to stand before a magistrate. Not once. I'd dissolve into a puddle. The law's a terror, your honors. Besides, I can't go against either liar since one of them is going to become my master—if I'm lucky enough to have one at all."

Ko wanted to argue with Shao-sing, but Hsi-wei stopped him.

"What do you say we all have some tea? Would that be possible?"

The old man said he had some freshly made and went

inside the villa to fetch the pot and three cups.

When they were settled, Hsi-wei spoke to Shao-sing gently, with respect, but to the point. "I'm told your son, your daughter-in-law, and your two grandchildren were tenants of the honorable Mr. Chin."

"That's true. The kind master rented the land to them for my sake"

"Well then, what if they owned that land?"

"What?"

"If, as I have reason to hope, we can win our case against Cao and Lu—"

"I can see that you know little of the world, young man. They're big men, rich. The law's made for the likes of them."

"With respect, at least one of them must lose; however, I think both will lose, as both deserve to. And, if they do, then you'll be free of both. In fact, if you help with the case, there's no reason why you and your family shouldn't move in here, into Mr. Chin's villa, as its new owners. Wouldn't that please you? Wouldn't that be worth the risk?"

The old man gawked at Hsi-wei, then turned to Ko.

"Who's more deserving?" said Ko. "And just think how your son will bless you, how your grandchildren will dote on you. Think how your daughter-in-law will wait on you!"

After Ko rushed off to the capital, Hsi-wei busied himself with making a few inquiries in the marketplace where he took orders for straw sandals and worked out how, if Ko succeeded with Xun, he would manage the hearing.

Six days later, a triumphant Ko returned with a sworn statement from Xun declaring that he had been hired first by Cao and then by Lu to prepare the two false wills. "I am a scribe," his statement concluded, "whose services are available to all."

The hearing was set to begin in the morning. Hsi-wei arrived in the borrowed official's gown. Cao and Lu entered the magistrate's court promptly, each accompanied by two witnesses, all former servants of Mr. Chin. Cao and Lu looked determined and angry; the four witnesses trembled and avoided looking at one another.

The bailiff pounded the butt of his pike on the floor three times and called the hearing to order. The magistrate entered through a high door and, with dignity, took his seat on the dais. He proceeded to take two scrolls from the wide sleeves of his yellow gown, the false wills. Speaking gravely, he reviewed the facts of the case. Looking first at Cao and then Lu, he reminded them that, as they had been informed, a delay had been granted when a stranger presented himself promising new evidence. With the authority granted by himself, that stranger, Mr. Chen Hsi-wei, would be serving the court as an examiner.

Hsi-wei stood before the dais and gave a low bow.

"Thank you, sir, for granting the delay and permitting me to pose some questions. It shouldn't take too long."

Hsi-wei turned around and asked which was Mr. Cao.

"Over here," Cao barked impatiently.

Hsi-wei strode over to the landlord. Cao, a man of about forty, had sharp eyes and a pointed gray beard.

"Good morning, Mr. Cao. A few questions, if you please. Do you believe the document submitted to the court by your neighbor Mr. Lu to be a forgery?"

"Most certainly."

"And that his two witnesses, lamentably now unemployed, were bribed?"

"That's obvious."

"Thank you, sir."

Hsi-wei approached Mr. Lu, a short, fat man of sixty with a wide face. He looked as if he'd just swallowed a cup of vinegar.

"Mr. Lu, good morning. Do you believe the document submitted by Mr. Cao to be a forgery?"

"Clearly. It's just what the greedy rascal would do."

"And his witnesses bought?"

"Naturally, and probably cheaply."

"But, as you've just heard, Mr. Cao says precisely the same of your document and your witnesses."

"The difference is plain. Cao's lying and I'm not."

"It's the other way around, you old scoundrel!" shouted Cao.

"Very well," said Hsi-wei calmly. "So, we have two irreconcilable versions of the truth. But there is a third."

"What do you mean?" roared Lu.

"What did he say?" growled Cao.

"Obviously, the third possibility is that each of you is telling only half the truth. Mr. Cao, you are correct in saying that your neighbor is lying, but so are you, Mr. Lu. Both documents are forgeries and all four witnesses have—in their desperation—succumbed to temptation and fear. In fact, you both agree with me about one another. I make that two votes for double fraud and only one for either of you."

"But that's preposterous!"

"And offensive!"

"It might be a preposterous offense if we didn't have this statement." Hsi-wei drew a small scroll from the sleeve of his official's robe. "This is a sworn declaration from the calligrapher Oyuang Xun, former resident of Hsuan. Please note that it is officially stamped by the prefect of police in the capital."

Hsi-wei handed Xun's affidavit to the magistrate, who read it and frowned.

"This would appear to be conclusive."

"I agree, sir. But, that's not quite all," said Hsi-wei.

"What? There's more?"

"Yes, sir. We have now ascertained that Mr. Chin did not give his land to either of his neighbors. But we also know to whom he intended to give it. Indeed, so do these two honorable gentlemen."

"How's that?" asked the magistrate.

Hsi-wei nodded to Ko who left the chamber briefly and returned with their star witness.

"Sir, this is Shao-sing, loyal senior servant to the late Mr. Chin. He has something to say."

The old man was shaking and wringing his hands. "It was a dinner, Your Honor," he mumbled.

"What's that?" said the magistrate. "Speak up."

Shao-sing shuddered but pressed bravely on.

"It was a dinner, Your Honor. A good one, with both pork and fish."

"Never mind the menu. What about this dinner pertains to the case?"

"Well, Your Honor, you see the girl was sick and that's why I was serving, which usually I wouldn't do. Mr. Chin had invited Mr. Cao and Mr. Lu. They talked a lot about crops and rents, and the weather too. And they drank a lot of yellow wine."

"Get to the point, man."

"Yes, Your Honor. Well, you see, since they were eating and drinking so much, I was always being called to bring in more of this or that, especially more wine. And, because I was in and out of the chamber the whole evening, I couldn't help overhearing what was said."

"And what was said that has a bearing on the matter before us?"

"Well, Your Honor, you see, it was at this dinner that Mr. Chin told his neighbors that—being childless—he was going to turn the land over to the peasants when he died. That is to say, his tenants. He said he thought they ought to know."

Cao and Lu, who had fumed and grumbled with feigned indignation at Hsi-wei's questioning, scowled at Shao-sing's testimony and looked at him with disdain and fury. Finally, neither could contain himself.

"He swore he would give it to *me*!" insisted the one.

"To *me*!" cried the other.

At this, Hsi-wei turned to the magistrate, smiled, and delivered an eloquent shrug. Shao-sing looked around in distress. Ko barely stifled a laugh.

The judgment was delivered the following morning. Deeds would be drawn up for the peasants and, in accord with a suggestion Hsi-wei made privately to the magistrate, ownership of the villa would now be assigned to the family of Shao-sing. As for Cao and Lu, both were soundly rebuked by the magistrate and required to pay substantial fines.

Ko and Hsi-wei celebrated that night with a large meal and plenty of yellow wine. They were pleased with what they had done and with one another.

After a pleasant week's stay, Hsi-wei prepared to depart.

"A most satisfactory visit," said Ko. "It's been fun. You're the ideal guest, Hsi-wei."

"And you, the perfect host. And we managed something good. You can believe the traveler who says that such justice is rare. And I'm excited about your work, the huge new piece in particular."

"Your praise is a great encouragement to me. And our collaboration on behalf of Chin's tenants really was a special pleasure."

"About collaboration."

"Yes?"

"I've had a thought about collaboration."

"What?"

"If there can be *Shan Shui* painting, why not *Shan Shui* verses as well?"

"Why not indeed. That's a splendid idea!"

"I'm glad you think so," said Hsi-wei and handed a small scroll to Ko Qing-zhao. On it, he had written the poem that is known by the same title as the painting universally acknowledged as Ko Qing-zhao's masterpiece.

Autumn in the Yellow Mountains

Deep in a golden grove on the riverbank
a slender lady in a silken gown sits with her
maid.
Both look out at a drifting sampan; the
inattentive boatman has dropped his oar.
The lady holds her hand to her mouth.
If I were that boatman I too would fail
to see the laughing lady and her maid
among the vivid leaves and twisting boughs.
My gaze too would be fixed higher, on the
waterfall like molten silver, the crooked
Huangshan pines, the rocks upholding all.
Leaves turn and fall. We laugh and drift
and soon are gone. Mountains endure.

MY NEPHEWS AND NIECES WILL BOAST WITH PRIDE

Michael Coolen

As I leaned out a broken window of an ancient bus, soaking up the sights and smells of the landscape as we careened down a washboard road in West Africa, I whispered to myself, "My nephews and nieces will boast with pride that this was the place where Uncle Mike died."

Just three days earlier, July 2nd, 1973, my wife, Virginia and I had been in Philadelphia joining other Peace Corps volunteers gathering for a few days of orientation meetings prior to flying to The Republic of the Gambia, West Africa (hereafter referred to simply as Gambia.) Our orientation included many events, from fingerprinting to a very sobering discussion of the various diseases and deadly creatures we might encounter there. Ebola would not surface until two years later, but Gambia was the home of snail fever, tuberculosis, schistosomiasis, elephantiasis, river blindness, polio, smallpox, hepatitis A and E, meningococcal meningitis, hookworm, and rabies. It also had nine of the deadliest snakes in the world, including the green mamba, some pit vipers, and a cobra or two.

We were assured that we would most definitely contract Falciparum Malaria, the deadliest kind of malaria in the world; far worse than that wimpy Asian kind that Brit colonialists and tourists whine about. Falciparum Malaria kills about a million people in Africa every year. It's such a deadly disease that a statue of the mosquito was erected farther down the African coast thanking the mosquito for killing so many European invaders. "It could have been much worse," is inscribed on the statue.

To combat and control the symptoms of malaria, we were urged never to forget to take a once a weekly dose of Aralen (Chloroquine), a symptom suppressant medication. One still has malaria but suffers few if any symptoms. At the end of that session, we all took our first dose to make sure nobody was allergic to it, because the side effects of Aralen included difficulty breathing, hearing loss, ringing in the ears, blurred vision, diarrhea, nausea, vomiting, lightening of the skin, swelling of the lips or tongue, rashes, itching, disorientation, and fever. I think there were several more, but I forgot the rest. In any event, none of the volunteers had bad reactions to the Aralen, nor were any of us fazed by the list of life-threatening critters and diseases. Everybody remained committed to going to Africa.

We flew out of Philadelphia on a chartered Boeing 707 filled with PCVs bound for several African countries. There was enough excitement, alcohol, and rowdiness during the eight-hour flight to qualify as an air born rodeo. At one point, someone yelled that he could see a cruise ship out his window. All but a couple of passengers rushed to that side of the plane to look. If I'd had any money I would have gone out and immediately bought stock in Boeing, because the plane handled the sudden weight reallocation beautifully (though I thought I heard one of the pilot's yell "What the hell?" inside the cockpit).

After we landed, we learned that our connecting flight out of Dakar did not/could not/should not/dare not/would not arrive. So, Peace Corps Gambia hired a bus to take us to Banjul, a 9-hour journey instead of a 25-minute flight on British Caledonian Airways. When the bus arrived to pick us up, my first thought was that it looked a lot like it had been built in the 1940s and at some point been abandoned by the side of the road. There were holes in the fenders, doors, floor; it had several broken windows. I also noticed a lot of leather pouches hanging from the rearview mirror, so I asked Jill, one of the local veteran volunteers what they were.

"Oh," she responded. "Those are *jujus*. The driver went to an Islamic holy man who wrote sacred verses from the Koran on pieces of paper and wrapped them in leather packets. They guarantee the safety of the bus and its passengers."

Jill paused for a moment before continuing. A poker-playing professional had nothing on the blank look Jill gave me.

"Or," she continued," the *jujus* guarantee the quick and painless death of the passengers in case of an accident."

I couldn't tell if she was speaking from tragic experience or blowing smoke up my multi-cultural naiveté. She's lying about the jujus, I thought.

"You're lying," I replied.

At that moment, the bus engine roared to a start, soon settling into a kind of serial tubercular cough.

"Hop aboard, rookie," Jill said, pointing to a door that remained open the entire trip. "The safest place to sit is close to the door," she continued. "I hope you don't find out why." She then sauntered onto the bus and sat down next to the door.

Three hours after the bus arrived to take us to Gambia, it shuddered to a start, and we took off in a cloud of hope and dread.

Just eight months earlier in December of 1972, I had been a graduate student at the University of Washington majoring in Ethnomusicology (the anthropology of music).

Over a period of two years, I had studied African music, dance, storytelling, and drumming from visiting African musicians. As a result, I had come to love African culture, food, and music, and I planned to do doctoral research on some aspect of African music. My preference was to study traditional marimba music in Mozambique.

I was employed as a graduate assistant in the Archives of

Ethnic Music and Dance when one of my professors told me that the Peace Corps was looking for an ethnomusicologist to work at the cultural archives of the Republic of Gambia in West Africa (aka Gambian cultural archives). Rod was an expert on the traditional musicians, historians, and genealogists of Gambia known as "*griots*" (GREE-ohs). He had written his dissertation on the kora, a 21-string harp-lute played there.

When Rod told me about the Gambia position, I wasn't quite sure what to do. Gambia was not only over four thousand miles away from Mozambique, but I had no idea what research I might undertake there. Still, this was a tremendous opportunity to realize my dream of living and working in Africa on someone else's dime. Fortunately, Rod came up with a great idea.

"You can do doctoral research on the *xalam*," he said (the x is the letter for the uvular fricative, pronounced like the "ch" in Bach). The *xalam* is a small, guitar-like instrument in Gambia, and it is considered one of the prototypes for the banjo in the United States.

Since I was already playing fiddle in a bluegrass band (when I wasn't acting as a ticket taker and bouncer), the idea of researching the origin of the banjo sounded intriguing, as well as other cultural connections between West Africa and colonial America.

"You could work in the Cultural Archives there and do field research on your own time," Rod continued. He was willing to write me a strong recommendation for the Peace Corps position, having been a PCV himself a few years earlier.

I applied for the position and convinced my girlfriend, Virginia, to apply also.

I was excited to live and work in Africa, and Virginia was beginning a graduate program in primate studies at the UW, and she saw an opportunity to undertake research on the troupe of Red Colobus Monkeys at the Abuko Game Reserve outside the capital. So, we were both excited when we were accepted into the Peace Corps in May. To the sound of bluegrass banjo, fiddle, and guitar we got married at a friend's home in late June, hopped the plane to Philadelphia the next day, and now found ourselves careening down the laterite clay roads years of abuse and no maintenance had converted into bone-rattling washboards.

The bus driver, who was fortunately blind in only one eye, was driving as fast as the bus would go. This was necessary not only to help 'surf" along the top of the washboard ruts in the road, but it also guaranteed the instantaneous death of everyone on board in case of an accident.

I realized that if the bus was going slower when it crashed, some of us might survive for a while, and there was no medical help within an 8-hour flight. I pictured myself dying in agony waiting for help that would never come. I wouldn't want my nephews and nieces to suffer emotional damage from memories of me by the side of the road, screaming while hyenas ate me alive, though my loving nephews and nieces would milk it for all it was worth back in Seattle.

"Maybe she wasn't lying," I mumbled to myself. "I hope those *jujus* work."

The scenery out the window included baobab trees with branches filled with dozens of vultures that seemed to be looking down at my bus. I began to worry that the vultures knew something about this bus that I didn't. I began looking for avian sabotage, wondering if maybe the vultures had dropped a dead gazelle on the road ahead in order to cause a wreck. Vultures are ugly but very resourceful.

Looking out past the vultures, I saw people waving at the bus from the doors of their huts with the traditional cone-shaped roofs. There was a red haze in the air, caused by the iron-rich laterite dust thrown up the bus rocketed down the washboard. Joy and fear and wonder and excitement and the unknown all rattled along in my brain in time with the rattling of the bus. I still couldn't quite wrap my mind around the idea that I was in Africa. I was more excited than afraid, perhaps because I was still safe on a bus traveling faster than mosquitoes and hyenas and snails and snakes and crocodiles, et al. But it was more than just the transient safety of an unsafe bus. I felt…free. And this sense of freedom calmed me.

As I looked out the window, I recalled the short but wonderful poem "*Ozymandias*" by Percy Bysshe Shelley. For me, it had always been the perfect response to the hubris of anyone seeking fame and some ever-lasting legacy. All that was left of the legacy of Ozymandias, king of kings, was "the long and level sands stretch[ing] far away." Nerd that I was, it also amused me, as the bus traversed the African bush, to recall that Shelley's middle name means "bush."

Late that afternoon, we finally skidded into the ferry landing at Barra, where the ferry crossed at the mouth of the Gambia River to Banjul, the capital. I jumped out of the bus and ran towards a local restroom…well, concrete hut that advertised itself as a restroom…and I immediately began re-considering if I really wanted to walk in my flip-flops through a two-inch thick muck of feces and urine to get to what appeared to be an overflowing toilet. After I described the bathroom facilities to Virginia, she suggested we wait until we'd crossed the river.

"Easy for you to say," I grumbled. "You have a stainless-steel bladder."

Including the time spent adrift when the ferry's engine cut out (a common event), my bladder arrived at the Atlantic Hotel ninety minutes later. As Virginia and I settled into our room on that first night, we learned the importance of netting designed to discourage mosquitoes big enough to stand flat foot and look a crow in the eye.

I found myself reviewing how the bus trip had taken me forward into Africa and backward in time. Self-delusion vanishes quickly in an Africa that is just too big, immediate, and overwhelming with challenge and promise. I found myself thinking differently about life, about my research, realizing that my plans for a glorious prize-winning dissertation were dimming in importance.

My little academic pretensions were meaningless compared to the scope of Africa. My realization that I was insignificant was a kind of liberation. Whether I completed my research or not, I felt readier than ever to do my research. I knew the results were relatively unimportant, except to me. I had begun one of the greatest adventures of my life, and I realized with great calm and a sense of great freedom that the process of the adventures to come was far more important than my survival of those adventures.

"My nephews and nieces will boast with pride that this was the place where Uncle Mike died," I whispered before I went to sleep, knowing I was ready for whatever came next.

What came next was two weeks of orientation, language training, three prophylactic rabies shots, personal health care suggestions (including writing out a will if you happen to suffer appendicitis if you are "in the bush"), and cultural sensitivity training that included a bus trip up-country.

And then, my work began.

LOVESICK WALRUS TURNS UP ON ORKNEY BEACH

Valerie Nieman

> *"He's probably come from Greenland or the west coast of*
> *Russia …I doubt he will find love here. It's bad enough for*
> *humans on North Ronaldsay."*
> —*The Daily Record and Sunday Mail*

Farms consider each other
across the wind-flattened grass;
inside the houses, people do the same,
pondering the half-empty marital bed.

Squabbles take years to clear:
people so few, so close,
you cannot afford to fight
but cannot help it.

Things cannot move on.

The skies promote sleeplessness.
Auroras suffuse the winter nights;
in summer the fallen sun kindles clouds
from below the horizon.

The beam from Stevenson's tall lighthouse
makes its rounds over land and far out to sea,
beware, beware this low ground
ringed with reefs and skerries.

A hard place to come aground, this,
a harder place to call home.

North Ronaldsay, Orkney

TOUCHED BY THE (TUSCAN) SUN

Olga Pavlinova Olenich

There are two flights of stairs to climb before I reach the apartment. The stairs are wide and cool and lost in darkness except on the levels where an occasional window lets in a weak yellowish light which washes across the honey-colored steps, hollowed out after more than a century of use. My new Italian shoes slip in the hollows, and the climb is hard work on a hot Tuscan day. I get to the familiar paneled walnut door with its curious black markings and find it open, but Damian and Peter are not at home. This comes as somewhat of a relief, a bonus, an invitation to throw off my shoes and dance through the spacious rooms on polished parquetry floors, skid near the narrow stairs and then climb out onto the roof-garden, to sit cross-legged among the terracotta pots which for the last two weeks have been spilling over with summer's gaudy geraniums. Sometimes I lie on the mattress I have put out there while the nights are hot and starry. This roof is more than 'A Room with a View.' This is a new horizon. From here I can look out over the piazza where the Henry Moore reclines, incongruous and impertinent on a circular patch of bright green grass, challenging the mellow façades of the old buildings. As I lean over the crumbling balustrade and see the pink terracotta roofs stretched for miles under a cloudless blue sky, I feel that particular surge of spirit that makes me breathless with the realization that I am where I am. In Italy.

This morning I went to Florence. The bus ride is one of my little joys. The local bus takes a willful and unnecessarily circuitous route through the impossibly narrow streets and often gets caught in the crazy Florentine traffic, shuddering and gasping and coming to a stop like some beached whale. However, I love every minute of it. It's not as if I am a driver negotiating my way, hot and impatient and volatile with deadlines and destinations to meet. I am the passenger, the sponge in the back seat, soaking up the delights of a daily journey that somehow defies the tedium of habit and leaps from scene to scene, from face to face, from sound to sound in an unpredictable kaleidoscopic way. I travel alone.

⎯⎯ ✦ ⎯⎯

I've been living with Damian and Peter for almost four months now and doing very little which could be deemed work except for giving the occasional private ballet lesson that pays extraordinarily well. I think it's got something to do with my Russian name and the reputation I have acquired in this small town on the outskirts of Florence. At first, the locals were very suspicious of me. A woman moving in with the two Australian gays. Not very Catholic. From under brows furrowed with disapproval, they gave me dark looks as I passed them in the street and they glowered like grey Venetian gargoyles when I came into their shops or ate in their restaurants. In a place where everyone seemed to have a name or designation, and the piazza rang with cheery greetings like "*Ciao Dottore!*" or "*Ciao Carissima!*" I remained nameless. Who was I? They were uncomfortable in addressing me. When the word eventually got around via Guido the hairdresser that I actually was a *povera signora* recuperating from a serious illness in Bella Italia, things changed dramatically, almost operatically, you might say. Where I was once met with the flat and reticent, "Buongiorno," to which I had become inured, I was now assailed by cadences and trilling accompanied by wild waving and much smiling and the unrestrained gesture of open arms ready to take me in and suffocate me with kindness. Pure Rossini.

The illuminating revelation about my health left an

afterglow that hovered over me like a halo in a baroque masterpiece. Once I had been cast as the ailing heroine, it became impossible to stick to the quiet daily pattern I had established. For instance, I began the day with breakfast in the little bar near the bus stop where the young waiter used to try to chat me up under the amused urbane green-eyed gaze of the elegant middle-aged patron. These days when I get to the bar, usually at about 8.30 while Damian and Peter are still asleep, the patron rushes to the door, solicitous and respectful, chats on about the weather and the news, compliments me on my clothing, and pulls out a chair. He is too delicate to ask directly about my health but searches my face for secret signs with the concern of a doting papa.

"A couple of months and she's everybody's darling," says Damian in his bitchiest voice but he is secretly proud of me and far from averse to embellishing the Signora's story. I hate to think what kind of life-threatening malady he has cooked up for me. Sometimes, I get floral tributes of proportions that make me suspect he has gone a teensy bit over-the-top. He and Peter are quite disarming in the very shamelessness with which they reap the rewards for being the Angels of Mercy, a role into which they have flung themselves enthusiastically, but only in public. Privately, I'm the healer, and they're the patients. But the public is fooled. Already my two bêtes noir, if you are allowed to have two, are more popular than they've been in the seven years of residence they have clocked up here, and the invitations flow in as steadily as the Arno wends her way through beautiful Florence. Every night we have to make decisions about which we can accept.

"Christ! The ***'s! They *own* the city! How did you meet them?" Damian is always the most scathing about important people, but he is the first to accept their invitations and puts us through hell when he's "getting ready." Once he is satisfied with his toilette, Peter and I get the once-over. "You can't be serious!' he groans, looking us up and down with fierce seagull eyes. "They'll think we're peasants!"

On one occasion we made the mistake of taking Felicity with us. We made the mistake of taking Felicity, full stop. Felicity was a friend of mine. Before leaving Australia, I had talked Felicity into meeting me in Italy. She was a dental nurse, very charming in a prim Englishy sort of way and very married. I thought the break from her family, not to mention the impact of Italy, would do her some good, widen her horizons. A few weeks ago while I was in Venice, Felicity appeared in Prato. I take my time-out in Venice. When the vases start to fly with the malicious velocity of the accusations and when things get so that no amount of maternal wiping of the brow can bring the boys' temperatures down, I grab my overnight bag and head for Florence station. A few quiet days in magical Venice at my favorite hotel in the room with the deep bath and the deeper window overlooking a minor canal, a few early morning walks through the piazza before the hoards descend, a bowl of hot mussel soup in the evenings at a little table in the restaurant downstairs, and I am ready to listen to their pathetic entreaties and extravagant promises over the telephone. I usually return to platform five in Florence on the fourth or fifth day when the guards are ready for the spectacle Damian and Peter are so expert in staging at regular intervals. My departures and arrivals on these occasions bring the platform to a halt. The guards delight particularly in the departures when the boys put on a truly gut-wrenching show in the belief that I am abandoning them for good. "Ah, signora! Signora!" intone the guards, wringing their hands but scarcely containing their pleasure. "*Che succeso? Che succeso?*" knowing full well '*che succeso.*' I settle down in the carriage with a sigh of relief and ignore the curious stares of strangers in the compartment who are being treated to the spectacle of Damian and Peter running alongside my window, gesticulating madly and mouthing wild promises that are, mercifully, lost in the sound of the departing train.

Having traveled across the world to be with "dear Ollie," Felicity expressed surprisingly little regret at my absence and did not, as Damian insinuated she might like to do, follow me to Venice. Instead, she cooked the lads a fabulous meal, showed them many photographs of her "cherubs"—the round-faced boy of about eight and the string bean of a girl a little older—referred to her husband as the "dear old thing," and made herself comfortable in my room. About as comfortable as a Giorgione cherub on a pink cloud. By the end of the week, she had made a good half-dozen of the ragazzi who regularly came to see Damian and Peter pretty comfortable in my room, too, according to an outraged Damian, himself the paragon of virtue whose entourage of local boys drives Peter to whisky and fits of despair as black as you'll get in any opera.

My homecoming was not a comfortable one. Felicity pretended to be overjoyed to see me but there was insincerity in her eyes, and her eyeliner had taken on a disturbingly bold Nefertiti line. Peter took me aside and asked how long she was going to stay. Damian took me aside and said she was a slut. And then "love" struck.

We had been invited to a wedding, the local doctor's niece was marrying into a prominent Florentine family complete with a "*castel*" and famous vineyards scattered over the hills in the Chianti district. With a generosity like flowing wine, the invitation spilled over to our visitor. I was nervous. After two weeks of amorous adventures, Felicity looked like hell. "We've got to get her to Guido's," said Damian, pulling in air between clenched teeth and releasing it with a threatening hiss. Guido runs a rather glitzy salon just around the corner. He has done wonders with my hair and is besotted with Damian. On this occasion, Guido excelled himself. Felicity's blonde hair, a great drawcard in Latin climes, was lightened further, puffed and blown and made glorious under the master's touch. I was ever so slightly jealous but reminded myself that I was several years younger and could afford to be understated. Actually, we made a rather elegant foursome—pastel linens and silk scarves all around. Damian was pleased with us, and we set off in relatively high spirits for people who were not all that keen on weddings.

———— ✦ ————

The newlyweds were a nice enough pair. I did not feel the urge to speculate on their future as they left the church. I suppose I reveled in their moment. There is enough of the romantic left in me, after all. I looked around at the guests and found them staid and disappointing. The priest, however, was young and dangerously engaging. Once I noticed this, I couldn't keep my eyes off him. However, when he saw me watching him and began to react, I recoiled. Unlike Felicity, I was not looking for love. I was recovering. Unrequited and impossible would be good for me, but this explicit acknowledgment from a man of the cloth would not, I suspected, be at all healthy.

"Damian!" I whispered, "The priest is flirting with me."

"Luscious, ain't he? When you've finished with him, I'll have a go."

We drove to the reception. The sun was setting behind the hills, and soft streaks of its last pink light drifted over the Chianti road. The lines of cypresses were black-green sentinels lining the street all the way to the twelfth-century castel where the wedding banquet was to be held. Like a white cloud left over from the day, the bride drifted out of an impossibly large black car and onto the mellow pink and orange terrazzo in front of the weathered and mossy walls of the old building. We followed her into a dazzling hall where elaborately framed portraits of her husband's ancestors looked over the festivities with an aloof disinterest painted into their features by artists working in the shadows of the old masters. It was the night of the brilliant chandelier and the living who were unquestionably triumphant. To our delight, it turned out to be quite some night. It must have been quite some night for Felicity too, or so we surmised because somewhere between the speeches and dances she disappeared.

———— ✦ ————

Damian and Peter were scathing when I expressed some anxiety the following afternoon. Damian, predictably, had one or two unspeakable ideas about what he thought might be happening to Felicity, one of which involved the gorgeous priest. That night there was a phone call.

"Ollie," said a weak and tremulous voice, which I barely recognized as Felicity's, "I know that you're not going to approve, but I couldn't help it. You have no idea what it's like to fall in love." The object of love, a certain Marcello, had been, as they used to say, "waiting table" at the reception. She told me they were off to Perugia. Marcello was, of course, no ordinary waiter. He was a student at the University. He had an aristocratic background. His family had never loved him. Damian was poking angry faces at me. He was dying to hear. She said that *they* (already a couple in word as in deed) would drop by in an hour or so to collect her things.

"Love!" screeched Damian, "Love!"

"A student!" chortled Peter, "a student!"

"From Perugia!"

"Why, what's wrong with Perugia?" I asked, genuinely confused. I had nothing against Perugia.

"Don't you know *anything*? It's where all the foreign students go. There's a whole army of Marcellos hanging out waiting for a free ride. How much money d'you think the old Felicity has with her?"

Marcello oozed into the door behind Felicity. His eyelashes were that much too long, his mouth that much too full-lipped, his expression just that much too self-absorbed. I loathed him on sight. While Felicity was packing, he hung around the kitchen where I was attempting to make pancakes. Like the large pancakes slipping around the pan, Marcello slid from wall to wall, thumbs in the front pockets of his very tight jeans. His murmured comments weren't memorable except for their appalling banality. When he slid up behind me and touched my hair, I was tempted to put the heavy fry pan to better use, but Felicity appeared just in time to save her true love from permanent disfigurement.

"Pretty boy," commented Damian as I led the lovers to the door.

"R*ee*-volting!" I hissed. Peter laughed. I hoped that Felicity would remember that the "dear old thing" and the cherubs were expecting a glad reunion with wife and mother in London at the end of the month.

At the end of the week, she was back. She looked the worst for the wear, and her eyes were puffy. The Nefertiti line had lost some of its precision under a cascade of tears. There had been a lover's quarrel. Afraid of missing the call of reconciliation from Perugia, she refused to leave the apartment, permanently draping herself over the couch from which she could easily reach the receiver. Her ostentatious misery drove me and Peter to drink and Damian to excessive verbal cruelty. But she did not react.

Eventually, a call did come for her. It was the "dear old thing." Surprise, surprise, he had managed to get away from work early, and at the very moment, he and the cherubs were safely ensconced in his sister's home near Oxford and simply *dying* for mummy to join them! They would not take no for an answer and were quite prepared to join her in Italy if that was what she wanted. The wailing could be heard in the piazza until Damian threatened to hit her in the face with a wet towel. To this, she reacted. Quite a sensible thing to do, I thought. For a few minutes, there was an uncomfortable silence. "I just have to see him." She burst into wild sobs. We gave her a glass of gin and promised to take her to Perugia the next day.

Damian woke up in a foul mood. He did not want to go to Perugia, but he didn't want to miss out, either. Felicity took the front seat with Peter who was driving the 2CV, borrowed from Guido. It had green plush velvet covers on the seats. Guido had been an upholsterer before he turned his hand to hairdressing. It was hot. The velvet stuck to the back of my knees and gave off the odor of old hairspray. Damian sulked and stared out of the window. I wished I had never persuaded Felicity to join me in Italy. A bit late.

"I was meant to live in Italy," she was saying to Peter.

As we neared Perugia, Peter asked for directions. "Where exactly does Marcello live?"

"I don't know, exactly."

"What do you mean, *you don't know*?"

"We weren't staying at his place."

"Where the hell were you staying, then?"

"In the Brufani Palace."

"The Brufani Palace! How much did that set you back?" Damian was aghast and jealous. Nobody had ever shouted him a room in the Brufani Palace. "Honeymoon suite, was it?" I decided to intervene.

"Felicity," I said in the firmest tone I could muster, "how on earth are we supposed to find Marcello? Don't you have a phone number?"

"Not really." Damian nudged me in the ribs. We began to giggle. Felicity sniffed. "He'll be easy to find. He'll probably be in one of the cafés near the university. It's not such a big place, you know."

Perugia was a lot bigger than I remembered. It was teeming with foreigners, and the Italians all looked like Marcello, or so I decided an hour after we had strategically separated to scour the city for Felicity's lost love. I went back to the piazza and found myself an outside table in one of the more popular places. My search was over, and so it seems was Peter's.

"Hey, Ollie!" His familiar figure emerged from the depths of the café.

"How long have you been here?"

"Oh," he said smiling quietly, "I came here immediately. Couldn't see the point of rushing about. We're just as likely to spot him here." We ordered coffee, and Damian turned up barely ten minutes later. He had been looking up an "old friend," but it was not an auspicious day for reunions. Occasionally, we thought we could see Felicity in the milling crowd, but it was hard to tell. There was no lack of fair foreign women "of a certain age" in Perugia, and there were legions of Marcellos.

The day was ending. Having consumed too many cups of coffee, mountains of gelato and several lunches, we were suffering from a peculiar form of hysteria brought on by the tedium of playing "Spot the Marcello" non-stop for the better part of a day. The waiters who had been quite amused at the beginning of our game were getting pretty sick of us. By five, we were the only ones who thought it screamingly funny to identify every passing man as the lost Marcello. It was time to leave. We had decided to meet Felicity on the steps of the university. To our surprise, she was there and had been for over an hour. She was very quiet. There had been no romantic reunion, not even a sighting.

I received a letter from Felicity yesterday. She is attending Conversational Italian classes at some school of languages along with a whole lot of other Australian women who are hoping to return to Italy and reclaim their Marcellos. Could I be cruel enough to write back and tell her not to bother? Marcello has reappeared in Florence. For the past week, he has been seeing more of Damian than he should. The rows here have been earsplitting. My overnight bag is packed.

THE ACCIDENTAL PEACEMAKER
Mary Donaldson-Evans

Ah, Norway! Land of deep blue fjords and majestic mountains, an ecologically-minded nation where goats graze on green roofs and urbanites ride their bikes to work, a country where any occasion is an excuse to bring out waffles with clotted cream and jam. In Norway, even trolls, the ugly creatures of Nordic mythology, are sold as cuddly toys, and the Vikings, Norse seafarers who pillaged their way through Europe for three hundred years, have become romanticized by history. Significantly, perhaps, Norway is the country where the Nobel Peace Prize is awarded, the only one of the six Nobel Prizes not to be awarded in Sweden, by the terms of Alfred Nobel's will, drawn up during a period when Norway and Sweden were ruled by the same king.

For all these reasons and more, my husband and I were smitten with Norway. It was thus with great excitement that at the end of a two-week cruise of the Baltic, we decided that we simply *had* to extend our stay in Bergen, Norway's second largest city. After some hesitation, for it was pricey, we booked a day-long excursion that would include three train rides, a bus transfer, and a catamaran cruise through the Nærøyfjorden, one of the country's most stunning fjords and a UNESCO World Heritage Site.

We left Bergen on a cool October morning, taking a local train to Myrdal. The ride took us through tunnels, past crystalline lakes, forested mountains shrouded in mist, turbulent mountain rivers. Wood frame houses with dormer windows dotted the hillsides. We felt as if we were living a fairy tale.

At Myrdal, we exited the train and crossed the platform to

the historic Flåmsbana (Flåm Railroad). This railroad, completed in 1944, had the steepest incline of any normal gauge railway in Northern Europe, descending from an altitude of 866 meters down to two meters, to the town of Flåm. If upon entering the train, we were charmed by its wood-paneled carriages, rounded ceilings, and deep red upholstery, we were dismayed to discover that all the window seats had already been taken. We slid into middle seats alongside a couple we would have recognized as British even if their canvas bags hadn't been festooned with small union jacks. Seeing the woman give me a sideways glance, I smiled at her. She did not return my smile.

The man sitting opposite her, ostensibly her husband, had horn-rimmed glasses, thinning grey hair, a bulbous nose, pendulous lips. Late sixties, I'd say. As for her, she was plump, had cropped "blond" hair and small eyes, and her soft, lined face was covered with post-menopausal down. They looked at each other with disdain. Whatever spark had originally brought them together seemed to have been extinguished long ago.

I assumed she'd lean back occasionally to allow me to point my iPhone camera at the stunning scenery we would soon be gliding past. It wasn't long before we began to move, and the countryside, already pretty on the run from Bergen, grew even more poetic. The hills gave way to snow-capped mountains and gushing waterfalls. Here and there a house painted in a shade of deep burgundy provided a spot of color in the pale-yellow autumn foliage of the birch trees and the poplars. I had heard that Norway was beautiful, but never did I expect such heart-stopping natural splendor. I simply had to capture this radiance, had to possess some photos to help transport me in spirit to this earthly paradise in the stressful days that I knew were ahead of me.

The couple were utterly oblivious to my need, leaning towards each other and almost completely blocking my view. I was vexed. If at least they had been enjoying the scenery, I would perhaps have been more forgiving, but they were engaged in an argument the subject of which I couldn't fathom. Their heads were turned slightly away from me, and they spat out their words in low voices.

"I *told* you," she hissed to her husband, her lips barely moving.

"But you didn't…" he growled, looking out the window, the rest of his utterance swallowed by the swishing and creaking of the old train.

"Because every time I tried to, you acted so bloody irritated…" she charged.

The staccato-like exchange continued, angry and accusatory, but I could make out only a few of the words.

Then: "So I suppose 5,300,000 Norwegians were wrong…" said the man, turning slightly away from the window so that I could see his face. Heavy bags seem to have ballooned under his eyes, and mockery and dislike were etched into his features.

"You are such a know-it-all," said the woman, turning away from him and looking straight out the window, gasping as she took note for the first time of the dramatic scenery unfolding before her eyes. She began snapping pictures, but when the train came to a stop at a lookout point opposite a roaring waterfall so that passengers could get off the train to take photographs, it was he who exited with his camera (an actual camera, not an iPhone) while she stayed in the car.

I returned to my place before he did. Noticing that she was wearing hiking boots, I asked her, "Going trekking?"

"Hardly!" she sneered, barely looking at me. Her tone did not invite further questions.

He returned to his seat, and for the next fifteen minutes or so, they clicked away wordlessly. However, she did lean back from time to time when she saw me struggling to take pictures that would not have them in the foreground.

Emboldened by this small act of kindness, I decided to try

to engage her in conversation.

"Have you noticed how few reds there are in the Norwegian fall foliage?" I asked.

She grunted. Apparently, she hadn't, or if she had, she hadn't found it significant. I pressed on:

"They mustn't have any maple trees over here."

Silence.

A bit worried that she had found my comment offensive, I continued:

"It's not a criticism; it's an observation."

Still nothing.

Then she looked at him, and he held her gaze, a smile playing about his lips. Her expression softened, her eyes twinkled. In some strange way, my intervention seemed to have redirected the mutual scorn that poisoned the air between them.

They were enjoying a private moment together. It was one of those meaningful glances; a shared thought transmitted silently by people who have lived together for so long that they no longer need to articulate their thoughts.

Damned Americans, it said. *They can never resist invading your space, smiling and trying to chat you up.*

HOMESICK
Matthew Mitchell

Watching a   small screen   bathed in orange swallowing
the sunset   outside   my bedroom I want
to say I love my father   like the   nine-year-old version
of myself did   my thin-fingered   hands waving
taking   deep   breaths   in the December air,
sticky with   saliva   cheering on our beloved team
a lineage which craves its   own collapse   while we were
surrounded by partitioned stadium seats   Southern
transplants   daughters of the Cuyahoga burning
but I am now the child of Hope Memorial Bridge
                            descendant of gas and dust
everything I touch   hands coated in dark matter
slowly collapses   the moonlight's pull   the ocean's
forgiveness   the sun dissolving beneath its crystalline skin
all creep down my cheek like a dog's   bark against
the capillaries wrapping around my   father's vertebrae
                            in another state

During the   coronation of my rustbelt self   an alchemy
of flames   and constellations   singe the edges of
the   television set   a hunk of swollen offense runs
 deep into the winter dark   where they invent
some bellowing dance   aching away another Sunday
 waiting for   a parade down Euclid

(This could, like always, finally be our year)

Tonight   I am a thousand miles south of him

watching rows of   pale orange seats lean into
the sunset   and tonight   the thinness of
Texas fireflies   are teaching me how
flooded with yells our Ohio yard   was and I can hear
his voice calling from   the living room *Come out here, son*
            Come watch the game with your old   man

But yet   in the farlight of the moon
just as I plead to the onscreen   snow falling
come back   come back   come back   where it
hides in the   gaps of a dim sunslant   the space
like a hand   splashing at the surface of
the Lake   our long distance séances amass
            gold watches   and   scoreboards
all of them out of time

ALME

Michael C. Keith

The desert has its secrets, and some are wonderful.
—Curtis Frederick

Word reached Acyl Kabadi that his father was gravely ill. At once, he prepared to make the journey to Koro Toro, sixty-seven kilometers from his tiny village in the deep Sahara. His twelve-year-old son, Ngia, would accompany him on the trek that would take them four days on foot. They had no other means of transportation since their camel had recently been stricken with lungworm. Given that their neighbors were about to depart for the bazaar in Oum-Chalouba, there was not one to be borrowed, either.

Before the sun rose above the flat horizon, they set out, leaving Ngia's mother, Dyese, and sister, Achta, to join the other villagers on their thrice annual sojourn to the marketplace. There they would peddle their handmade jewelry and leather goods and purchase essential supplies for the coming months.

By noon the next day, Acyl and Ngia had traveled far into the Djourab basin. It was there that the sky lost its color, stained by swirling sand. As they made their way across a stretch of dunes, the wind intensified and soon their visibility was lost.

"We will stop and shield ourselves, my son. Come, let us gather in until the storm is over," shouted Acyl, who fought to wrap his body in a white kaftan he planned to wear when greeting his father. "Ngia!" he called again, but there was no answer, as his son was beyond the reach of his voice.

The strong blasts of sand stung Ngia's face and drew tears to his eyes as he called out for his father. The only thing either could hear was the din of the ferocious *haboob*. Ngia was no stranger to the Sahara storms, but he had never experienced one as powerful as the one that now separated him from his father.

Ngia formed into a ball and burrowed into the dune to keep from being battered. There, in the darkness, he waited out the storm, hoping it would soon end and he could find his father. Despite shielding himself, Ngia found that the insidious sand had made its way deep inside his mouth. He attempted to spit, but he had no saliva and, when he swallowed, it felt as if stones were lodged in his throat. His breathing became so difficult that for a time he thought he would suffocate.

Just as things seemed hopeless, the sand and wind settled, and Ngia dug himself from the dune and scoured the landscape for signs of his father. Everything had been transformed by the storm. The dunes had been reconfigured, making his surroundings appear unfamiliar. Ngia was disoriented and had no sense of the direction in which he and his father had traveled before the dusty onslaught.

"Baba!" called Ngia until his parched throat gave out.

There was no sign of his father as he carefully searched for him from atop the highest dune he could mount. His thirst was growing, but he had not carried water. At least his father would have something to drink, and that thought comforted Ngia as he removed sand from his eyes, ears, and nostrils.

The sky remained the color of the desert. As long as the sun was concealed, Ngia could not get his bearings to return home or continue to the place of his ailing grandfather. By the time the sky had cleared, and the sun was visible, Ngia had decided to press on with his travel to Koro Toro. It would be what his father would do, and he believed his parent would wish him to do likewise. He fervently hoped they would meet along the way.

———— ✦ ————

It was nightfall when Ngia reached the edge of the dunes and was able to move without his feet sinking into the sand with every step. Although the solid ground would allow him to move more swiftly, he was exhausted from hours of dragging his legs through the mounds of sand. He located a large rock and nestled against it, unaware it was home to a family of foxes. As quickly as he went to sleep, he was awakened by something licking his feet. He let out a scream, and a baby fennec scooted away. Ngia decided to find another place to sleep, quickly locating what he thought a more suitable resting area next to a large Welwitschia plant. Its leaves felt cool against Ngia's skin, and he promptly returned to his dreams.

Before the sun rose, Ngia was awakened by ant bites on his neck and legs. He leapt to his feet and frantically brushed the insects from his body.

"Baba!" he called loudly as he moved away from his infested bed.

There remained no response to his desperate summons. As the eastern sky brightened, Ngia began to move in the direction of what he hoped would take him to his grandfather's home. He had never felt such thirst, and he experienced tremendous weakness as he walked across what would soon be a blistering surface.

"Baba, baba," he muttered, stumbling more than striding.

It was not long before what little energy he had was gone, and he collapsed to the desiccated soil. When he struck the ground, his hand touched something strange, and he pulled it away anxiously. After a moment, he dared to make contact with the object again. It reminded Ngia of a dried goat stomach that his mother made into carrying pouches, but it felt coarser. As Ngia lifted his head for a look, he became dizzy and lost consciousness. When he came to, cool water was washing over his body.

"Baba, baba!" he bellowed, expectantly, but when his eyes cleared, he beheld an elephant.

At first, he was frightened, but then he recalled a favorite story told by a village elder in which a man had touched the skin of a deceased elephant only to have it come to life and grant him a wish. The man had asked for the ability to sire children, something he had not been able to do, and soon he and his wife were blessed by a dozen offspring.

"Tembo, please find my father," pleaded Ngia, and the pachyderm lifted him to its back with its trunk and carried him away.

From his elevated perch, he soon spotted his father and directed the elephant to trumpet a signal to gain his attention. The loud sound startled Acyl, who then returned his son's excited wave.

"Where did you get this wondrous animal, Ngia?" asked his father, looking up at his son.

"It is like the tale, Baba. I touched the skin, and it appeared," explained Ngia. "Climb up with me, and we can travel to see dear, sick Oupa."

The elephant extended its trunk to Acyl and lifted him to his son. When it was dusk, they alighted and spent the night amid a cluster of date palms. In the morning, they discovered that the elephant was gone. A piece of its skin lay on the ground where it had stood the night before. This alarmed both Acyl and Ngia, for they felt it was a sign that their fate would hold further sorrows.

"Baba, look!" shouted Ngia, pointing toward the south.

"It's Koro Toro," declared his father, relieved.

Ngia rolled up the piece of elephant skin and tucked it beneath his darija. He and his father then set off for the town, which they calculated was less than six kilometers away.

"Will grandfather die?" asked Ngia.

"He is very ill, and the healer is no longer able to make him well, my son."

———◆———

When Acyl and Ngia arrived at the elder Kabadi's mud-brick dwelling, they were shocked and delighted to find him sitting on its doorstep, looking robust.

"Oupa, we feared you were dying," said Ngia, befuddled.

"No, no," laughed his grandfather. "I found magic to heal me. Look," he said, removing an object from his cloak and setting it on a small wooden crate.

"It is my elephant skin!" exclaimed Ngia, searching his clothing for it. "It is gone, Baba! It is not where I kept it!"

As he spoke, it began to rain hard—something very much out of season. The Kadabi's rejoiced for the wonderful relief it provided them. When the refreshing cloudburst ended, they noticed that the elephant skin had vanished.

Grandfather, father, and son stared in amazement at the crate where it had been only moments before.

"*Magic* tembo," declared Ngia, with a broad grin, and the jubilant Kadabi's sang songs of praise and thanks as another wave of cooling droplets descended from the cloudless sky.

LOCATION SLUTS
Joan Frank

"The author divides her time between…"

Paris and Santa Barbara. San Francisco and Tuscany.

Portland, Maine, and Kealakekua, Hawaii. The New Hampshire woods and Manhattan.

Yeah, yeah. Los Angeles and Tahiti. Positano and Cape Cod. Bozeman and Tokyo.

God, how I hate these declarations: often the final flourish in an *About the Author* bio, generally found on the backs of book jackets or at the ends of articles. I mean no disrespect, but—really. Don't you at least briefly hate these, too? Or at least raise an eyebrow?

Quickly: what's your first thought, viewing such claims?

Mine snaps down like a mousetrap:

Well, how delightful. It only falls to the rest of us wretched peasants—we who've just one home—to envision the Author relishing this stately division.

Of course, certain presumptions are built in: lucky-devil Author has earned or inherited or married or partnered a financial instrument sufficient to arrange Living The Dream. (Occasionally: Author lives and works in Y, partner lives and works in X; the couple migrates back and forth.) More subtly, such biographical glitter suggests that the author has carefully chosen what she/he holds to be the two best possible places on earth—and the best times of year for living in each of them.

Are you, reader, presently nested in either of those places? No? Ah, too bad for you, then.

End of story.

Except, not. The casual report of two homes in two locations sets rolling, in a reader's mind, a little caravan of unwanted thoughts that begin wandering off in different directions like a loosed herd of confused moose. First thoughts might be envious: *Gee, I wish I could live that way, too.* Other thoughts might mosey into a dark forest of dismay, in which the reader accuses herself of not having done so well—not paid the right kind of attention, not acted prudently or shrewdly enough, failed to sell film rights—whatever it would have taken to afford setting up and squatting in two homes in two fabulous locales.

A friend once insisted that when you return from an extended trip, you have about ten minutes to clearly see your own surroundings for what they are. Generally, the impression makes you wince: endearing, but funky. Slightly shabby, if lovable. Those back-door stairs—splintery. That front porch plank, sagging deeper. When did the paint wear off the wainscoting? How did the windows get so dirty; the screens so nasty? And yikes, those smudge marks.

Jacket flap declarations ("divides her time between...") have a way of waking our personal ten minutes of clarity with a small crack of lightning—kind of like the *Bride of Frankenstein*—every time we read them.

Maybe most authors don't give a damn about what gongs are struck in a reader's head when they view these graceful claims. Possibly the authors hardly think about it or assume the material gets ignored. Maybe they didn't write it themselves; maybe their publicists did.

Interestingly, I've known people with two homes. Sometimes one home is seasonal: a summer retreat, untenable in winter. Either way, to me the reality of owning two places sounds...unsettled. How, I've wondered, could you really feel situated—as the British say, *sorted*—if you must have two of everything, keep two of everything in good repair, and relatedly, realized too often that your favorite version of the desired thing (clothing, shoes, tools, pills, sporting goods, kitchen paraphernalia) is stowed at the other place? (The *other place* will inevitably acquire a name, shorthand for easy reference: "The Cabin," "The Apartment," "New York" "Shangri-La.") I've also wondered about the costs and effort of maintaining two venues: houseplants, pets, bills, mail, and routine domestic chores. I think as well of the strange, human, greener grass syndrome: feeling pulled toward the other property, no matter where you may presently be camped. (Is it Tolstoy or Chekhov who depicts a character longing for the *dacha* once installed in the city, then immediately craving the pied-à-terre after removing himself to the country?)

Does the above qualify as sour grapes? As a way of telling ourselves, "since we can't afford such luxury, let's find reasons to decide that it's a crappy way to live?"

I can neither confirm nor deny.

Let me distract you at this point with a game my husband and I never tire of playing. It often starts while we're in motion, staring at other locales: walking, driving, in a plane or on a train.

If we could afford it, the game always begins—quickly appended by, "if Joan were able to sell film rights to one of her novels," followed by Joan's swallowing hard—*which place would we like to live in, part of the year?* Where would we just flat-out buy a house or cottage or apartment, because we are pretending we absolutely could?

This is a hella delicious game. Convenient. Gratifying. It costs nothing. It risks nothing—nobody else knows we're doing it; therefore we court no judgment, no contrarianism, no scorn. Best, it's wide-open as the sky. All options are feasible; money's no object. And for a festive bonus—since husband and self have internalized each other's habits and natures—a pre-established hierarchy of biases and prejudices automatically clicks into position. We're in heated agreement.

Assumption one: No wintering. We don't do cold.

Assumption two: Blue and green. That's code for natural beauty. Only world-class cities (London, Paris, Rome, New York) may be semi-exempt from the blue-and-green criterion. And even they, thank God, through handsome parks and appending countryside, may offer precious slices of it.

Assumption three: Humane, arts-loving, *simpatico* vibes. A diversity of ages, ethnicities, demographics. A dash of whimsy, of playfulness, wouldn't hurt. (France is good at that, believe it or not.)

The rest of our preferences are easy to predict. Vibrant culture, physical ease, access to healthy food. No sense listing various talismanic places here—everyone has their own such list. Then, depending how exercised we've become, we go through our list of contenders, venue by venue, and unpack each one—and ultimately (wait for it) decide why each choice is perhaps finally *not quite* the bulls-eye choice: why in fact it's probably better (freer, cheaper, easier) just to rent some space in that place whenever we feel like it, rather than buy outright. Soon we pretty much forget about even renting there, and we feel better yet. Think of all the money and heartache we've just saved! Realtor's fees! Gasoline! Guilt for not being wherever we aren't!

Then we resume the lives we're leading—a little lighter around the heart, sighing with refreshed clarity—noticing too, with brighter pleasure as we go about our days, the abundance of particulars that make us happy about where we actually live.

As I say: all this costs nothing, except some thinking and talking. And the reward's real: renewed gratitude and appreciation for our present humble set-up.

Here's a cousin-game to the above. Though it involves gusts of imagination, it feels effortless while in progress. As reliably as a tapped knee causes a shin to kick, whenever we visit an attractive city or town we immediately begin to think, in the course of exploring it, *Hey, We Could Live Here.*

It's the damnedest phenomenon.

We begin to stare with great urgency at the layouts of neighborhoods, conditions of houses, downtowns, and landscapes fore and aft. We start counting up cafes, libraries, theaters, parks, schools, ethnic eateries; qualities of public transport, ratios of trees to streets. We search people's faces (for expressions of contentment); we size up their general bearing and *bien-être*. We have gone so far as to drop in at the local Chamber of Commerce to collect a packet of informational flyers intended for new residents, usually titled Welcome To Our City.

Weather figures, naturally. All the elements named in the pre-established hierarchy figure. In our minds, rapidly, we set up a Typical Day in the New Location. We picture ourselves beginning that day holding a cup of excellent coffee, likely standing at a big, clean window, gazing out to the lovely lawns and fir trees (or the orange and lemon trees, or papaya and banana, or the desert cacti, or the exciting, hipster-urban center several stories below us) that we've so long admired. In no time our eyes start to shine, our voices to quicken, as each item on our list of necessities seems to be checked. *We could ride our bikes from home to the library, and to coffee. Terrific coffee! Bookstores! Food trucks! We could subscribe to the Little Theater. Take or teach classes. I'm sure there's a gym here somewhere. How pleasant these streets, this park, this art museum!*

And then—at first slowly; then rather fast—we forget about it.

Other tasks tug at our attention. If the adored city is part of a tour, we carry on visiting different cities and towns, where similar, whirlwind romances flare up. Like children freshly fixated on a new toy, we swiftly shed the last fixation: the town or city where, mere days or weeks ago, we'd meticulously begun to plot to spend the rest of our lives. We seldom look back.

What confounds me is how easily this happens: how lightly we float away from what began as something close to passion. My guess? That it's the intangibles, the unseen furnishings, and assets of our present setting, which make themselves felt and call us back—with very little conscious awareness on our parts. Those intangibles include a deeply entrenched network (small but sturdy) of friends. None of them is Einstein, but most are thoughtful and kind. Most have known us so long that the simple fact of their nearby presence—the embedded understanding of their automatic, earnest support—seems at this point to help flesh out our own comprehension of ourselves. Were we to yank up stakes and drop them elsewhere, it could take, we sense, quite some long time to meet and make new friends—to move past the pleasant-novelty-of-contact phase into a state of genuine friendship. At our ages, that chunk of time signifies. Other familiarities fan out for review: patterns of movement, proximity to other cities where we have family, other longtime friends, and other pleasurable patterns. All these considerations urge us, paraphrasing Fagin's immortal words, to "think we'd better think it out again."

It might not, after all, be the most enviable state—touching down by turns in two communities, without meaningfully belonging to either.

Perhaps, of course, that's not always the case.

And yet.

This game, by the way, is called *Location Sluts*.

Might it look impressive, do you think, in a biographical statement?

MR. O'BRIEN'S LAST SOLILOQUY

Robert Garner McBrearty

We came back from the war and we were just rolling along for a while, all through the fifties, like there was nothing but good times ahead. One of my happiest memories is standing in dirt. The good dirt in our back yard. Our new house. We'd had a smaller house, but now there was another kid on the way, and we got the new big house. Everything felt new. The whole neighborhood was new. Brick houses. Ranch mostly. But all of them a little different. Not like today.

We'd pitch the caliche over the back yard into the alley. All of us. Mary, me, the kids. It was something we did together. We pitched it over the fence. Cleaning it out so the grass would grow. All of us in the yard and throwing the lumps of caliche over the fence. Standing in the dirt. In our backyard. Our home. There was something I did only when I was alone, after we got the kids to bed. I'd go out in the yard, and I'd patrol it. I'd walk the fence line. Sometimes I lay down on the dirt when it was dark in the yard and nobody could see me. I lay down in the dirt and I stared up at the stars and I said to myself, this is all right, this is mine.

We went to a school play once, when Len was in kindergarten. He had a role where he had some kind of magical dust sprinkled over him. He lay down on the stage. He was supposed to roll over now and then to show he was dreaming. But every time he rolled, he got closer to the edge of the stage. There was a big drop-off, four or five feet or so. He kept getting closer to the edge. You couldn't tell whether it was part of the play or whether he really was asleep and he was going to roll right off the edge of the stage and break his neck. I was a wreck watching him get closer and closer. I almost jumped out of my seat.

The sixties came along, and it was like the world blew up in our faces. The Bay of Pigs, the Cuban missile crisis, J.F.K. Right here in Texas. I heard things at the office. A couple of men I'd considered friends, men I'd liked, over at the water cooler, they were talking about how Kennedy got what he deserved, he couldn't come down here telling us what to do. I fired them. I fired both of them right on the spot. I told them to get the hell out of the store.

Then I sat in my office and I cried. I'd never fired anybody before, not unless they were stealing. He was our president. And in Texas. Right here. On our watch. It made me sick.

I thought it was Oswald acting alone. I don't know anymore. I don't know what to think. Mary never agreed with me. The C.I.A., she thought, the Mafia, Castro, the Ku Klux Klan, she would get these ideas in her head and she wouldn't let them go. He didn't act alone. She must have said that a thousand times until I wanted to tear my hair out.

I don't know why it upset me so much when she said he didn't act alone. I guess it was like, well, if he didn't act alone, who could you trust?

Everything was changing. The blacks and their marches. Mary said of course they're marching. Why shouldn't they march? I'd march too. I hired a Negro in the accounting department. He was the best man for the job, so I hired him. You'd have thought I turned a shark loose in the store. They hated him, and they were mad at me for hiring him, and I guess I was relieved when he came to me and said, I'm sorry, Mr. O'Brien, it's not working out for me here. Mary told me I should have stood up for him more. Mary was right about a lot of things. You never know things until it's too late.

I smoked like crazy back then. Mary did too. We all smoked. Why didn't it kill me the way it killed Mary? I wanted it to be me, not her, if it had to kill somebody. I knew I was supposed to quit. We all knew. That's baloney that we didn't know.

The bad things just kept coming. It was like you couldn't get over one thing before something else hit. Vietnam. Bobby Kennedy, Martin Luther King. The kids going wild. The hair, the drugs. My own sons, hair down to their asses. Why did it get on my nerves so much? I should have just let it go. And it's nothing compared to today. You see it all now – green hair, purple hair. Rings through the nose. The lips, the eyes. Nice looking black girl comes in to help me to the toilet the other day and she opens her mouth and she's got a silver hoop through her tongue. That's all new.

Len was a good kid. Sure, some trouble here and there, but a good kid. Then they called him up for his own war. One war in the family was enough. Mary told him he wasn't going. She was going to make him go to Canada. But what could we do? If I could do it again, I'd take him to Canada myself. You never know things until it's too late.

Everything's new. I'm not even sure if this is the same country we fought for. The other day I woke up and I thought: I don't even know if this is America anymore. Maybe this isn't a country at all anymore. In a real country, you've got a goal. You've got a purpose. You're working together. You're building for the future. You want to make the world a little better for your kids.

What's our purpose now? I'm not sure I see a purpose anymore. People are just walking around talking on cell phones and buying things or shouting at each other on the television.

If you asked me what I believed in, I'd say kids. Sure, kids. Your own kids, then you get the grandkids, now there's the great-grandkids. I can't keep them straight, who is who. I don't think they know who I am either, but my grandkids, and I'm not even sure about all their names either, push them at me and say, go give Pa-Pa a hug. I scare them, in my wheelchair, but I like the hugs. I'll take what I can get. Pa-Pa. I get a kick out of that.

I got so little time with my own kids. I was always working. When you are ninety-four years old, I will tell you one thing you will not regret. You will not regret that you didn't work more. It's always too late. By the time you know anything, it's too late. Maybe you can warn people not to make the same mistakes. Not that they'll listen. But here it is, if you want to hear it.

Don't work so damn hard. Spend more time with your kids. And throw your kid in a closet and tie him up before you let him go off and get killed in a war. Because in the end, you're the only one who will care. You and your family. The country will survive without your kid. You're the only one who will miss him every day for the rest of your life.

I didn't expect all these years to keep running by. After Mary went, I wanted to follow. But the heart keeps beating, the lungs keep breathing. It's a new day, a whole new ballgame. What's with all the machines to keep you alive? What's the point? There comes a time to call it quits, bag it in.

Time. I wouldn't want to be young again. One time through is enough. I wouldn't mind being eighty. I was still going strong at eighty. I walked five miles a day. But if I was eighty, I'd be missing Mary all over again. After she went, I tried to walk away the pain or it was like I wanted the pain to be somewhere else, to be in my hips or my back or my feet, anywhere but the pain eating away inside.

Funny, Mary is closer to me again. I can't explain it, but I see her a lot now. That girl with the hoop in her tongue rolled me into the bathroom and I saw her in the mirror, standing behind my chair, and for a minute she looked just like Mary, different color and all, but she still looked like Mary, and I said, Mary, just like that, Mary, and she bent over and she hugged me and she said, that's okay, honey, that's okay now.

Bon Voyage!

CONTRIBUTORS

Michael C. Keith is the author of more than 20 books on electronic media; an acclaimed memoir, *The Next Better Place*; a young adult novel, *Life is Falling Sideways*; and fourteen story collections—*Of Night and Light, Everything is Epic, Sad Boy, And Through the Trembling Air, Hoag's Object, The Collector of Tears, If Things Were Made To Last Forever, Caricatures, The Near Enough, Bits, Specks, Crumbs, Flecks*, and *Slow Transit, Perspective Drifts Like a Log on a River, Let Us Now Speak of Extinction,* and *Stories in the Key of Me*. He was a finalist for the National Indie Excellence Award and the International Book Award and has been nominated ten times for the Pushcart Prize, as well as *The Best American Travel Writing* series and the Pen/O.Henry Award. Website www.michaelckeith.com.

Nicholas Litchfield is the founding editor of *Lowestoft Chronicle* and author of the suspense novel *Swampjack Virus*. He has worked in various countries as a tabloid journalist, librarian, and media researcher. He writes regularly for the *Colorado Review* and his book reviews for the *Lancashire Post* are syndicated to twenty newspapers across the UK. He lives in western New York. Roam his website at www.nicholaslitchfield.com.

Rob Dinsmoor is the author of three fictive memoirs, *Tales of the Troupe, The Yoga Divas and Other Stories*, and *You Can Leave Anytime*. He also co-authored the children's picture book *Does Dixie Like Me?* His story collection, *Toxic Cookout*, is forthcoming from Big Table Publishing. He lives on the North Shore of Massachusetts. Website www.robertdinsmoor.com.

A faculty member at the University of North Carolina School of the Arts, **Joe Mills** has published six collections of poetry, most recently *Exit, Pursued by a Bear*.

Elaine Barnard's stories and plays have won awards and been published in *Lowestoft Chronicle, Kyso, Red Fez, Zimbell House, Sunlight*, and many other literary journals. She has been a finalist for Glimmer Train and Best of the Net, and was nominated for the Pushcart Prize and Best Small Fiction. Her collection of stories from her travels in Asia is forthcoming from New Meridian Arts. She received her BA from the University of Washington, Seattle and her MFA from the University of California, Irvine.

Douglas Cole has published four collections of poetry and a novella. His work appears in *The Chicago Quarterly Review, Chiron, The Galway Review, The Pinyon Review, Solstice, Eastern Iowa Review, Kentucky Review, Wisconsin Review*, and *Slipstream*. He has been nominated for a Pushcart and Best of the Net, and has received the Leslie Hunt Memorial Prize in Poetry; the Best of Poetry Award from Clapboard House; First Prize in the "Picture Worth 500 Words" from Tattoo Highway. His website is douglastcole.com.

M. T. Ingoldby works as a copywriter in the UK. His stories have appeared in *Litro, Pennsylvania Literary Journal, Lowestoft Chronicle, The Next Review, Existere, Octavius Magazine, Crimson Streets, Story and Grit*, and one or two anthologies, working his way up to a novel. He is an active member of the Waterloo Theatre Group and a keen runner. He currently lives in London.

Retired after four decades' prizewinning print and broadcast journalism in Hartford CT, **Don Noel** received his MFA in

Creative Writing from Fairfield University in 2013. He has since published more than three-dozen short stories and non-fiction pieces, but has two novellas and a novel still looking for publishers. Most of his work is available at his website, www.DonONoel.com

Robert Perron lives and writes in New Hampshire and New York City. Past life includes high-tech and military service. His stories have appeared in *The Manchester Review*, *Sweet Tree Review*, *STORGY Magazine*, *Adelaide Literary Magazine*, *The Fictional Café*, *Front Porch Review*, and other journals. Visit his website at https://robertperron.com.

Jean L. Kreiling's first collection of poems, *The Truth in Dissonance* (Kelsay Books), was published in 2014. Her work has appeared widely in print and online journals, including *American Arts Quarterly*, *Angle*, *The Evansville Review*, *Measure*, and *Mezzo Cammin*, and in several anthologies. Kreiling is a past winner of the *Able Muse* Write Prize, the Great Lakes Commonwealth of Letters Sonnet Contest, two New England Poetry Club prizes, and the *String Poet* Prize.

David Macpherson is a retired internal medicine physician living on a small farm in western Pennsylvania. He retired in 2016 as a Professor of Medicine from the University of Pittsburgh and as a Chief Medical Officer for the Veterans Health Administration serving as the lead physician in a mid-Atlantic region. His work has appeared in *Scarlet Leaf Review*, *Adelaide Literary Journal*, *Front Porch Review*, and *Rind Literary Magazine*, and the *Pittsburgh Quarterly*.

Matthew P. Mayo is the award-winning author of thirty-plus books and dozens of short stories. His novel, *Tucker's Reckoning*, won the Western Writers of America's Spur Award for Best Western Novel, and *Stranded: A Story of Frontier Survival*, won the prestigious Western Heritage Wrangler Award for Outstanding Western Novel, the Spur Award for Best Western Juvenile Fiction, the Peacemaker Award for Best Young Adult Western, and the Willa Award for Best Historical Fiction. It was also a High Plains Book Award Finalist and Will Rogers Medallion Award Finalist. Mayo has been an on-screen expert for a popular TV series about lost treasure in the American West and has had three books optioned for film. He and his wife, photographer and videographer Jennifer Smith-Mayo, run Gritty Press (www.GrittyPress.com) and live in the deepest, forested wildlands of Maine. Rummage around his website (www.MatthewMayo.com) for updates about spurious projects and outrageous outings.

Diane G. Martin was awarded first prize at Lunch Ticket's Diana Woods Memorial Award for Creative Nonfiction, and has published poetry, prose, and photography in numerous literary journals including *New London Writers*, *Lowestoft Chronicle*, *Vine Leaves Literary Review*, *Poetry Circle*, *Open: Journal of Arts and Letters*, *Breath and Shadow*, the *Willamette Review of the Liberal Arts*, *Portland Review of Art*, *Pentimento*, *Twisted Vine Leaves*, *The Examined Life*, *Wordgathering*, and others. Diane has traveled throughout much of the world. The themes of exile, disability, and displacement pervade her work.

Katie Frankel is a recent graduate of Texas Wesleyan University with a degree in English. She particularly enjoys memoirs and historical fiction, and, when not writing or reading, takes leisure in traveling and riding her horse.

Mark Halpern has lived since 1993 in Tokyo, where he runs his own law firm. He was born in America, mostly grew up in Canada, and has spent long periods in the UK and France.

In 2016, he began writing short stories about foreigners living in Japan. In life, Mark has done enough foolish things to be capable of granting his characters the same level of respect he grants myself. And, like some of them, in Japan he has found a way to be both an outsider and an insider.

James B. Nicola's poems have appeared in *Lowestoft Chronicle*, *Antioch Review*, *Southwest Review*, *Atlanta Review*, *Rattle*, and *Poetry East*. His nonfiction book *Playing the Audience* won a Choice award. His four poetry collections are *Manhattan Plaza*, *Stage to Page: Poems from the Theater*, *Wind in the Cave*, and *Out of Nothing: Poems of Art and Artists*. sites.google.com/site/jamesbnicola.

Brian James Lewis is an emerging writer of prose and poetry who is a member of the Academy of American poets. His work has appeared in *Third Wednesday*, *The Iconoclast*, and multiple issues of *Trajectory Journal*. His poem "Garage Sense" can be read on their site's editors picks section. Besides creative writing, Brian writes book reviews for *Hellnotes*, *The Horror Review*, and *Damaged Skull Writer*. When not writing, Brian repairs vintage typewriters. Keep up with Brian @skullsnflames76 on Twitter!

Philip Barbara's short fiction has been published by *The Delmarva Review*, *Fiction on the Web* (a July 2017 pick of the month) and *The Corvus Review*. His story "The Church" was adapted into a radio play by NPR affiliate Delmarva Public Radio. He and his wife live in Alexandria, VA.

Sharon Frame Gay grew up a child of the highway, playing by the side of the road. She has been published in several anthologies, as well as *BioStories*, *Gravel Magazine*, *Fiction on the Web*, *Literally Stories*, *Lowestoft Chronicle*, *Thrice Fiction*, *Literary Orphans*, *Indiana Voice Journal*, *Crannog Magazine*, and many others. Her work has won prizes at Women on Writing, The Writing District and Owl Hollow Press. She is a Pushcart Prize nominee. You can find her on Amazon Author Central as well as Facebook as Sharon Frame Gay-Writer.

Richard Charles Schaefer is a Massachusetts native living and writing in Chattanooga, Tennessee with his wife, daughter, and two cats. He recently finished his first novel and is working on a collection of short stories. He holds a BA in English and Political Science from Umass Amherst.

As a scribe, **Gary Singh** has published over 1000 works, including newspaper columns, travel essays, art and music criticism, profiles, business journalism, lifestyle articles, poetry and short fiction. He is the author of *The San Jose Earthquakes: A Seismic Soccer Legacy* (2015, The History Press), and was recently a Steinbeck Fellow in Creative Writing at San Jose State University. http://www.garysingh.info

Lawrence Morgan was born in Miami, raised in Istanbul, and left home at the age of 15 to have adventures. He has curated a private zoo for a Turkish industrialist, trained as a safari guide in Africa, and worked in the Hollywood film industry. He currently spends most of his time between Scotland and South Africa.

Thomas Piekarski is a former editor of the *California State Poetry Quarterly* and Pushcart Prize nominee. His poetry and interviews have appeared in literary journals internationally, including *Nimrod*, *Florida English Journal*, *Cream City Review*, *Mandala Journal*, *Poetry Salzburg*, *Poetry Quarterly*, *Pennsylvania Literary Journal*, *Lowestoft Chronicle*, and *Boston Poetry Magazine*. He has published a travel book, *Best Choices In Northern California*, and his epic adventure *Ballad of Billy the*

Kid is available on Amazon in both Kindle and print versions.

Dave Gregory was a young writer in search of the world when he inadvertently ended up with a career in the cruise industry. Two decades later, he has retired from life at sea and returned to his first love – writing. His work has appeared in *Eunoia Review*, *Soft Cartel*, and *Clever Magazine*.

Dan Morey is a freelance writer in Pennsylvania. He's worked as a book critic, nightlife columnist, travel correspondent, and outdoor journalist. His writing has appeared in *Hobart*, *Cleaver Magazine*, *McSweeney's Quarterly*, *Lowestoft Chronicle* and elsewhere. His work was nominated for a Pushcart Prize in 2017. Find him atdanmorey.weebly.com.

Matthew Menary lives in St. Louis County, Missouri, where he works as a cashier in a grocery store. He has lived in France, Hawaii, Missouri, California, and Japan due to a curious combination of being a homebody with a serious case of fernweh, a homesickness for the unexplored. He has one essay published in the anthology, *I Thought My Father Was God*.

Nebraska State Poet **Matt Mason** runs poetry programming for the State Department, working in Nepal, Romania, Botswana and Belarus. He is the recipient of a Pushcart Prize for his poem "Notes For My Daughter Against Chasing Storms" and his work can be found in numerous magazines and anthologies, including Ted Kooser's *American Life in Poetry*. The author of *Things We Don't Know We Don't Know* (The Backwaters Press, 2006) and *The Baby That Ate Cincinnati* (Stephen F. Austin University Press, 2013), Matt is based out of Omaha with his wife, the poet Sarah McKinstry-Brown, and daughters Sophia and Lucia.

Timothy J. Lockhart is a lawyer and former U.S. Navy officer who worked with the CIA, DIA, and Office of Naval Intelligence. He has published articles and book reviews in a variety of publications, including *Naval Intelligence Quarterly*, *Naval War College Review*, and *The Virginian-Pilot*. Stark House Press published his first novel, *Smith*, in 2017, and his second novel, *Pirates*, in 2019. He lives in Norfolk, Virginia, with his wife and daughter.

Robert Wexelblatt is professor of humanities at Boston University's College of General Studies. He has published the story collections *Life in the Temperate Zone*, *The Decline of Our Neighborhood*, *The Artist Wears Rough Clothing*, and *Heiberg's Twitch*; a book of essays, *Professors at Play*; two short novels, *Losses* and *The Derangement of Jules Torquemal*, and essays, stories, and poems in a variety of scholarly and literary journals. His novel *Zublinka Among Women* won the Indie Book Awards first-place prize for fiction. The story collection, *His-wei Tales*, and a collection of essays, *The Posthumous Papers of Sidney Fein*, are forthcoming.

Michael Coolen is a pianist, composer, actor, performance artist, and writer living in Oregon. In addition to three Fulbright Fellowships and four National Endowment for the Humanities Fellowships, he has won awards from the Oregon Poetry Association and the Oregon Writers Colony. His essay "Let Me Tell You How My Father Died" was awarded first prize in the 2017 national "Ageless Authors" competition. He has been published in dozens of journals and online publications. He is also a published composer, with works performed around the world, including at Carnegie Hall, New England Conservatory of Music, Museum of Modern Art, and the Christie Gallery.

Valerie Nieman's third collection, *Leopard Lady: A Life in Verse*, features work that has appeared in *The Missouri Review*, *Chautauqua*, *Southern Poetry Review*, and other journals. Her writing has appeared widely and been selected for numerous anthologies, including *Eyes Glowing at the Edge of the Woods* (WVU) and *Ghost Fishing: An Eco-Justice Poetry Anthology* (U Georgia). She has held North Carolina, West Virginia, and NEA creative writing fellowships. She teaches workshops at John C. Campbell Folk School, NC Writers Network conferences, and many other venues. Her readings have included the WTAW, Piccolo Spoleto, and Joaquin Miller series. Her fourth novel, *To the Bones* (WVU Press), came out in spring 2019. A graduate of West Virginia University and Queens University of Charlotte and a former journalist, she teaches creative writing at North Carolina A&T State University.

Olga Pavlinova Olenich is a widely published writer from Australia.

Once a professor of French literature, **Mary Donaldson-Evans** came down out of the ivory tower in 2011 and hasn't looked back. Her creative work has been published by *The New York Times* ("Metropolitan Diary"), *Lowestoft Chronicle*, *Diverse Voices Quarterly*, *Corner Club Quarterly*, *BoomerLitMag*, *The Literary Hatchet*, and *Spank the Carp*, among others.

Matthew Mitchell—a recipient of the Grace Chamberlain Prize in Creative Writing, the highest English honor at Hiram College, and the Richard C and Jo Ann Murphy Underwood Award for Journalism—is featured in issues of *Lunch Ticket*, *Clockhouse*, and *The Oakland Arts Review*.

Joan Frank (www.joanfrank.org) is the author of six books of literary fiction and an essay collection about the writing life.

Her latest novel, *All The News I Need*, won the Juniper Prize for Fiction. Joan's work has received many honors and awards, including the Richard Sullivan Prize for Short Fiction and two ForeWord Reviews Book of the Year Awards, one of them for *Because You Have To: A Writing Life*. She lives in Northern California.

Robert Garner McBrearty's short stories have been widely published, including in The Pushcart Prize, *Missouri Review, North American Review, Ellery Queen Mystery Magazine,* and previously in *Lowestoft Chronicle.* Robert is also the author of three short story collections and a novella, and he has received the Sherwood Anderson Fiction Award and fellowships to the MacDowell Colony and the Fine Arts Work Center. His forthcoming flash fiction collection, *Wake Me When I Can't Sleep*, will be published by Matter Press.

COPYRIGHT NOTES

Other titles in the acclaimed anthology series!

Lowestoft Chronicle 2011 Anthology
Edited by NICHOLAS LITCHFIELD

"This is a fine anthology that I found both provocative and enjoyable. Highest praise: it made me want to write short stories again."
—LUKE RHINEHART, author of the cult classic *The Dice Man*

"Michael Connor's 'Stevie and Louie' is a fun read about a young, single tourist in Austin…'The Shooting Party' by Jack Frey is a story of a chance encounter in an exotic location that is both plausible and mysterious. It makes good use of dialogue and an inventive plot."
—*New York Journal of Books*

"All things considered, it might just be a very good thing if the Lowestoft Chronicle were to achieve their goal of world domination."
—CHERYL LaGUARDIA, *Library Journal*

Far-flung and Foreign
Edited by NICHOLAS LITCHFIELD

"Hot off the press [is] this terrific anthology culled from Lowestoft Chronicle. The writing here is fresh, surprising, and alive. Not to be missed is the bittersweet interview with the author Augustine Funnell. (Please write more!) The book looks and feels great."
—NICHOLAS ROMBES, author of *A Cultural Dictionary of Punk*

"Nicely laid out…eclectic…humorous pieces with an emphasis on travel, hence many of the works take one to far-away and exotic places. I immensely enjoyed 'The Adventures of Root Beer Float Man' by Michael Frissore. For poetry, try Wayne Lee's 'Ordinary Deckhand.'"
—*Newpages.com*

"I've enjoyed reading the *Chronicle*. 'I Like Your Deer's Moustache, and other Lithuanian Tales' …[is] a distinctly Baltic twist on mistaken identity. One of our most popular pieces."
—*My Audio Universe*
(Rijn Collin's story aired on the independent radio station KVMR)

To order, visit www.lowestoftchronicle.com

Intrepid Travelers

Edited by NICHOLAS LITCHFIELD

"Without a single stinker or filler piece in the bunch. I was extremely impressed with the variety and quality of the writing. *Intrepid Travelers* is a solid collection of funny and fine travel-themed stories, poetry, essays and interviews that easily fits in a back pocket or carry-on bag."
—FRANK MUNDO, *Examiner.com*

"Many short stories and poems here offer deeper meanings and address heavier topics. 'Something Like Culture Shock' by Dennis Vanvick…[has] good character development and a compelling story. 'Political Awakening, 1970' by Denise Thompson-Slaughter…it was refreshing to read a piece with this much depth. 'Pájaro Diablo' by Michael C. Keith…by the end, the reader is riveted to see what will happen next. Also features an interview with Randal S. Brandt…[which] make[s] for an entertaining read. Overall, this is full of great talent and exceptionally written pieces."
—TARA SMITH, *The Review Review*

"Refreshing and well-written, *Intrepid Travelers* takes the reader to a wide variety of literary destinations, and makes even a confirmed hermit like me want to get up and go somewhere. Highly recommended."
—JAMES REASONER, *Rough Edges*

"Prepare for an adrenalin surge as a thief tries to escape from armed Mafia agents in Hector S. Koburn's fatalistic 'Bloody Driving Gloves,' Steve Gronert Ellerhoff's brilliantly quirky short story, 'Apophallation,' [and] Michael C. Keith's unexpectedly moving 'Pájaro Diablo.' *Intrepid Travelers* is a coruscating cornucopia of humour, drama and big, beautiful adventures. Highly original and entertaining."
— PAM NORFOLK, *Blackpool Gazette*

"It's unique and the quality of the writing is amazingly high."
—LUKE RHINEHART, internationally bestselling author of *Long Voyage Back*

Somewhere, Sometime...

Edited by NICHOLAS LITCHFIELD

"The latest collection of prose and poetry from the *Lowestoft Chronicle* is a genuine pleasure. Nicholas Litchfield has put together something very special, something to celebrate, enjoy, savor."
—JAY PARINI, bestselling author of *The Last Station* and *Why Poetry Matters*

"What a lovely book. Well designed, thoughtfully laid out, and with a grand assortment of content."
—MATTHEW P. MAYO, Spur Award-winning author of *Tucker's Reckoning*

Other Places

Edited by NICHOLAS LITCHFIELD

"In the age of tweets and sound bites, it's heartening to read *Other Places*, a publication celebrating the power and beauty of a story well told."
—SHELDON RUSSELL, author of the Hook Runyon Mystery series

"*Other Places*, a mouth-watering feast of short stories, poems, narrative non-fiction, and in-depth interviews, is the latest anthology from the much-admired *Lowestoft Chronicle*, an eclectic and innovative online journal. Packed into the pages are stories to entice, enthral, and entertain. Litchfield also serves up a tasty blend of pleasing and deftly prepared poems. And if you still aren't sated by this literary banquet, tuck into Litchfield's incisive and enlightening interviews with three critically acclaimed, multitalented writers."
—PAM NORFOLK, *Wigan Evening Post*

"I really loved the latest anthology from Lowestoft, *Other Places*. It's a brilliant, savory, sharp, amusing and varied taste of my favorite magazine, *Lowestoft Chronicle*. I'm delighted that a place exists for this kind of travel writing—if that's a term for it. And it's not a good one. This is just great writing about place, ranging from the spirit of place to the human spirit. Go anywhere with Lowestoft. And enjoy the trip."
—JAY PARINI, internationally bestselling author of *The Passages of H.M.*

"*Other Places* is the usual delightful mix of stories, poems, author interviews, and non-fiction gleaned from the pages of the *Lowestoft Chronicle*, the only literary magazine I read on a regular basis. Always entertaining and insightful, *Other Places* is well worth your time, whether you're a veteran traveler or a hermit like me!"
—JAMES REASONER, *Rough Edges*

"Armchair travelers, rejoice! Editor Nicholas Litchfield has released *Lowestoft Chronicle*'s anthology for summer 2015, *Other Places*. Filled with fiction, nonfiction and poetry about travel and destinations, the book brings the far corners of the world to the reader's armchair. The stories and poems vary in tone from dead serious to delightful whimsy, offering something for every taste. Humor, adventure and mystery share the pages with intriguing result."
—MARY BETH MAGEE, *Examiner.com*

"Sick of fly-by journalism and travel dilettantes? The antidote is *Lowestoft Chronicle*'s most recent anthology, *Other Places*—a collection of essays, stories, and poetry devoted to the in-depth experience of culture. Whether humorous, touching, or revelatory, these expertly curated pieces throw you in contact with the real."
—SCOTT DOMINIC CARPENTER, author of *Theory of Remainders*

To order, visit www.lowestoftchronicle.com

Grand Departures

Edited by NICHOLAS LITCHFIELD
Foreword by Robert Garner McBrearty

"The stories, poems, and essays in Nicholas Litchfield's latest anthology, *Grand Departures*, are haunting, idiosyncratic, and unexpected, like the true delights of travel."
—IVY GOODMAN, award-winning author of *Heart Failure*

"A must-have collection of travelers' delights and demons."
—NANCY CARONIA, contributor to *Somewhere, Sometime* and co-editor of *Personal Effects*

"An impressive collection of travel works that sweeps the reader across the globe."
—DORENE O'BRIEN, award-winning author of *Voices of the Lost and Found*

"It is fun, edgy at times, international in its scope. It surprises. The work is a blend of the serious and the comical, dark shades, light shades, and as I said, ever surprising."
—ROBERT GARNER MCBREARTY, author of *The Western Lonesome Society*

Invigorating Passages

Edited by NICHOLAS LITCHFIELD
Foreword by Matthew P. Mayo

"A powerful literary passport—this adventurous anthology is all stamped up with exciting travel-themed writing. With humor, darkness, and charm, its lively prose and poetry will drop you into memorable physical and psychological landscapes. Pack your bags!"
—JOSEPH SCAPELLATO, acclaimed author of *Big Lonesome*

"A wonderful collection from a fine literary journal. Fine writing that stirs the imagination, often amuses and always entertains."
—DIETRICH KALTEIS, award-winning author of *Ride the Lightning*

"*Invigorating Passages* delivers on all counts, hits on all cylinders too. The writing is skilled, the choices rich, the passages manifold, and the invigoration unfailing."
—ROBERT WEXELBLATT, award-winning author of *Zublinka Among Women*

"*Invigorating Passages* is a rare and dynamic literary collection which grabs readers firmly and sweeps them away to strange and exhilarating places, presenting intriguing situations, colourful characters, and making us yearn to strap on the backpack and go exploring."
—PAM NORFOLK, *Lancashire Post*

To order, visit www.lowestoftchronicle.com

CPSIA information can be obtained
at www.ICGtesting.com
Printed in the USA
LVHW041813291219
641998LV00001B/37/P